starting out in chess

BYRON JACOBS

D1469864

EVERYMAN CHESS

First published 1999 by Everyman Publishers plc, formerly Cadogan Books plc, Gloucester Mansions, 140A Shaftesbury Avenue, London WC2H 8HD

British Library Cataloguing-in-Publication Data
A catalogue record for this book is available from the British Library.

ISBN 1 85744 226 1

Distributed in North America by The Globe Pequot Press, 6 Business Park Road, P.O. Box 833, Old Saybrook, Connecticut 06475-0833.
Telephone 1-800-243 0495 (toll free)

All other sales enquiries should be directed to Everyman Chess, Gloucester Mansions, 140A Shaftesbury Avenue, London WC2H 8HD
tel: 0171 539 7600 fax: 0171 379 4060
email: dan@everyman.uk.com
website: www.everyman.uk.com

To Joshua

EVERYMAN CHESS SERIES (formerly Cadogan Chess)
Chief Advisor: Garry Kasparov
Advisory Panel: Andrew Kinsman and Byron Jacobs

Typeset and edited by First Rank Publishing, Brighton
Production by Book Production Services
Printed and bound in Great Britain by The Cromwell Press Ltd., Trowbridge, Wiltshire

Contents

Chapter One

How the Game is played

- The Attraction of Chess
- The Conduct of the Game
- The Board and the Pieces
- Getting to know Your Army

The Attraction of Chess

To the casual observer, chess can appear to be a terribly complicated game. Many games and sports are easily comprehensible to the non-specialist. Anyone interested in football can appreciate a brilliant goal, while tennis enthusiasts can marvel at a spectacular rally. Furthermore, in most events spectators can usually tell what is happening. Take golf and snooker. There are great subtleties to both games which can be debated at length by experts. However, the basic premise is understood by the casual observer and the keen enthusiast alike: if the ball goes in the hole (or pocket) it's good; if not, it's bad. What you see is what you get.

Chess is not so easy. Games played at a high level often turn on subtle technical points. These games may be fascinating struggles and generate beautiful ideas, but they are not easily understood by casual players who have not studied chess to a high level. This mystique helps to contribute to the charm of the game, but it is often difficult to explain why one player has the better position on the board or why the selection of a particular plan proved decisive.

So does this mean that chess can only be enjoyed after years of study and practice? Certainly not. It may take a while for the subtle play of the very best players to be understood but learning to play and enjoy chess is not difficult, as hundreds of millions of people around the world will testify. Chess is immensely rewarding in that it is easy enough to learn in a few hours and complex enough to be enjoyed for a lifetime.

One of the great attractions of chess is that all moves are, quite literally, 'above board' and are decided upon purely by the players themselves. This is not the case with many other games: in backgammon, a brilliant strategy can be undone in a flash by an unfortunate roll of the dice, while in bridge, an ingenious defence can fail hopelessly if an inattentive partner proves uncooperative. When you play chess you can see exactly what your opponent is up to and, conversely, you cannot conceal your own strategy.

Demis Hassabis from London is one of the world's most versatile games players, having won many competitions in games as varied as chess, Shogi, Go, Othello and Entropy. He expresses the beauty of chess succinctly: 'I think chess is the best arbitrary game. It has evolved over a period of many centuries and is beautifully balanced, with perfect interplay between the pieces. Meanwhile the complexity is pitched at a level which is finely tuned to the capabilities of the human mind.'

The Conduct of the Game

Chess is essentially a war game, played out on the battlefield of a chessboard. The two players control an army of pieces and decide upon how best to manoeuvre their forces. One player takes the white pieces and the other plays with their black counterparts. The player with the white pieces has the modest advantage of the first move (somewhat akin to being the server in tennis) and thereafter the players move alternately.

Only one move can be made at a time. A move is made by taking one of your pieces and placing it on a different square. When you have done this, your move is complete and it is your opponent's turn to move. You always have to make a move if it is your turn – passing is not permitted.

It is not possible to move one of your pieces to a square on which you already have a piece. Only one piece can occupy a square at any given time. However, if an opponent's piece is occupying a square to which one of your pieces can move, you can still make this move and in so doing you will capture the opposing piece. This piece is then removed from the board and will take no further part in the game. Unlike draughts (checkers), captures are optional and not compulsory. You can only capture opposing pieces, not your own. Once a piece is removed from the board, it is out of play for the rest of the game. In Shogi (Japanese chess), captured pieces transfer to the opposing side and can then parachute back down onto the board with dramatic consequences. This does not happen in chess.

Each player starts the game with 16 pieces: one king, one queen, two rooks, two bishops, two knights and eight pawns. The eventual aim of the game is to capture the opponent's king – to give checkmate. It is also possible – and, indeed, at a high level quite frequent – for the game to result in a draw.

In order to prevent players from taking too long to decide on a

move, almost all serious chess is played using a chess clock.
The chess clock is placed adjacent to the chessboard within
easy reach of both players. The classical form of this device is
actually two clocks, situated side by side. Only one of these
clocks runs at any one time. While it is your turn to move, your
clock is running. When you have decided upon your move, you
make it on the board and then press the button on top of your
clock. This stops your clock and starts your opponent's. Players
have an allotted amount of time to complete either the whole
game, or a certain number of moves. A player who exceeds
their time allocation is deemed to have 'forfeited on time' and
loses the game. The position on the board is irrelevant. You
may be winning and, indeed, be about to force checkmate, but a
time forfeit cancels this out and you lose the game.

The Chessboard and the Pieces

The battlefield for the game of chess is an 8x8 board of 64
squares, alternately coloured light and dark, as in diagram 1.

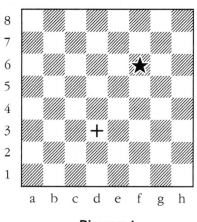

Diagram 1
The chessboard

Note the co-ordinates given along the left-hand side and lower
edge of the board. These act as a reference map to enable the
moves of chess games to be recorded. In general, literature on
chess omits these from diagrams, but in this book, to enable
the moves and ideas to be followed more easily, all diagrams
will have co-ordinates. Thus in diagram 1, the f6-square is indicated by a star, while the square marked with a '+' is d3.

Conventionally, the board is (almost) always shown from White's viewpoint.

In order to articulate ideas more easily, sectors of the board are given specific labels, and it is useful to be aware of these:

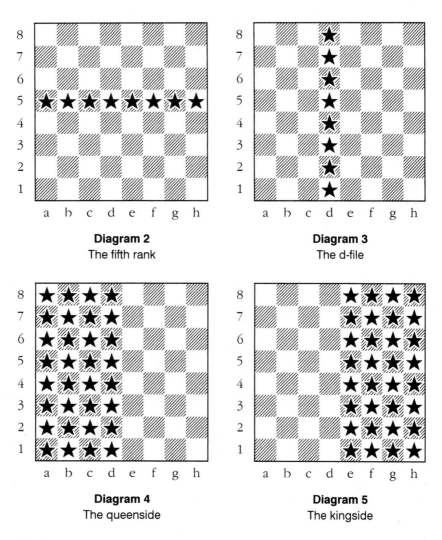

Diagram 2
The fifth rank

Diagram 3
The d-file

Diagram 4
The queenside

Diagram 5
The kingside

The lines across the board are referred to as ranks. For example, the fifth rank stretches across the board from a5 to h5 (diagram 2). The lines running vertically up the board are known as files. For example, the d-file consists of the squares running from d1 up to d8 (diagram 3). Additionally, the four left-hand files (i.e. the a-, b-, c- and d-files) are known collectively as the queenside, while the four right-hand files (i.e. the e-, f-, g- and h-files) are known collectively as the kingside (diagrams 4 and 5).

Getting to know Your Army

The pieces can be represented by either letters or symbols, as follows:

Piece	Letter	Symbol
King	K	♔
Queen	Q	♕
Rook	R	♖
Bishop	B	♗
Knight	N	♘
Pawn	P	♙

The queen and rook are the most powerful units and they are often referred to as the major pieces. The less mobile bishop and knight are known as minor pieces. A slightly confusing aspect of chess terminology is that although the pawn is obviously a chess piece, a reference to 'pieces' implies the queens, rooks, bishops and knights. For example, a typical chess comment is that 'White has active pieces but weak pawns'.

Diagram 6
The starting position

The initial position of the pieces is seen in diagram 6. White's forces are placed along the first and second ranks, whereas Black's are stationed on the seventh and eighth ranks.

Summary

Chess is essentially a war game. The two players control an army of pieces and have to decide how to best manoeuvre their forces.

Each player starts with 16 pieces: a king, a queen, two rooks, two bishops, two knights and eight pawns. These pieces all have different methods of moving.

The ultimate aim of the game is to checkmate the opponent's king.

Chapter Two

Meet the Pieces

- Moving and Capturing
- Check and Checkmate
- Piece Mobility
- Try it Yourself

Moving and Capturing

The chess pieces move in very distinct ways. Some have more mobility than others and this makes them more valuable. A fundamental aim in chess is to win material by exchanging your lower-ranking pieces for the opponent's more valuable ones, leaving you with a more powerful army on the board than your opponent.

The Rook

The rook operates along the ranks and files and can move any number of squares, as long as there are no intervening pieces. In diagram 1, the black rook has complete freedom of action to operate along the d-file or the eighth rank. In diagram 2 the white rook is more restricted, only being able to move as far as f4 along the third rank, and c7 along the c-file, where it would capture the black knight. The rook cannot 'jump' over intervening pieces, so the squares c8 and h4 are unavailable. The white rook could capture the black knight on c7 (the white rook would move to the c7 square and the black knight would be removed from the board), but the g4 square is currently occupied by the white pawn and is thus also unavailable. You cannot capture your own pieces.

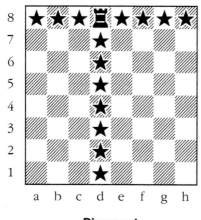

Diagram 1
The moves of the rook

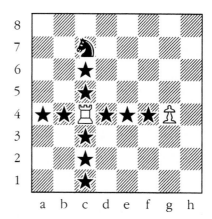

Diagram 2
The moves of the rook

The Bishop

The bishop operates along the diagonals and, like the rook, can move freely as long as there are no other pieces in the way. Thus in diagram 3 the white bishop can move to any of the squares a2, b3, d5, e6, f7, g8, a6, b5, d3, e2 and f1. As with the rooks, the bishops are not permitted to 'jump' over pieces. Thus in diagram 4 the black bishop, restricted by its own pawns, can only move to e7, g7 or h8. However, it is able to capture the white rook on d8. The bishops are permanently restricted to the colour of the square on which they start the game. Thus in these two examples, White has a 'light-squared bishop' while Black has a 'dark-squared bishop'. Each player starts the game with one dark-squared and one light-squared bishop.

Note: The bishop is the only piece which is unable to move to all squares of the board.

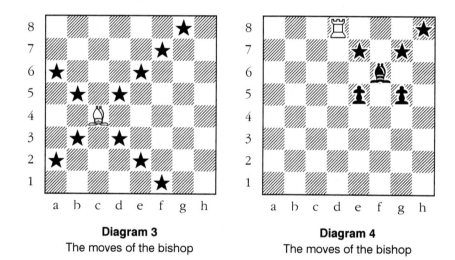

Diagram 3
The moves of the bishop

Diagram 4
The moves of the bishop

The Queen

The queen is the most powerful piece on the chessboard, as it combines the activities of both the rook and the bishop. Thus the white queen in diagram 5 can move to any of the marked squares and can also capture the black bishop on g8 or the black knight on d2. As with the rook and bishop, the queen is not permitted to jump over pieces and so the squares a2, b3, d1 and h1 are not available. Even when stationed in the corner, as in diagram 6, the queen is still very powerful, covering the furthermost squares in the three remaining corners of the board.

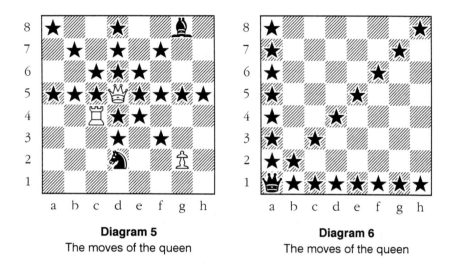

Diagram 5
The moves of the queen

Diagram 6
The moves of the queen

The Knight

Of all the chess pieces, the move of the knight is the one that causes most problems for newcomers to the game. It moves in an L-shape, two squares along any rank or file and then one square at right angles. Another way to perceive this is to visualise a 3x2 'box' of squares; the knight can move from one corner to an opposite corner. This movement is much easier to perceive from a graphical representation rather than a textual one. In diagram 7 the white knight can move to any of the indicated squares.

The knight is the only piece which is permitted to jump over intervening units. Thus in diagram 8, the pawns at c5 and d5 do not stop the knight from either capturing the white rook on d4, or from moving to b4 or e5. Other squares available to the knight are a7, b8, d8 and e7. However, as with all other pieces the knights cannot move to a square occupied by a piece from their own side. Thus a5, which is currently occupied by a black pawn, is out of bounds.

In comparison to a rook or bishop the knight appears to be a rather feeble piece. Rooks and bishops can sweep the length and breadth of the board with just a single move, whereas the knight is restricted to a local area. However, the unique ability of the knight to hop around makes it a very useful piece.

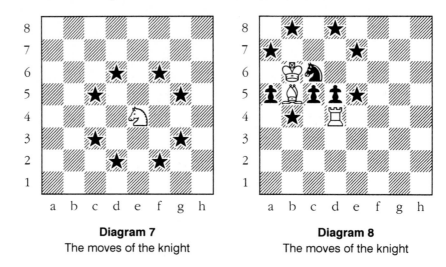

Diagram 7
The moves of the knight

Diagram 8
The moves of the knight

The knight is, without question, a difficult piece to handle. In order to get a feel for its movement, place one on an empty chessboard and move it on a tour in such a way that it visits all the squares along a rank, file or diagonal. For example, place a knight at a3 and then move it in such a way that it passes through, b3, c3, d3 and so on to h3. One way to start such a route is **a3**-b5-d4-**b3**-c1-a2-**c3**. This will help to give you an appreciation of the mobility of this tricky piece.

A peculiarity of the knight is that sometimes it finds it easier to move long distances than short ones. Consider diagram 9.

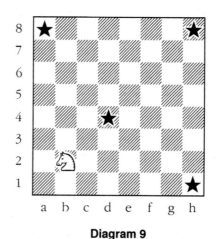

Diagram 9
A peculiarity of the knight's movement

Let's assume we want to relocate the knight from its current post on b2 to any of the indicated squares: the central d4, or the far-flung a8, h8 and h1. Which square would you expect it could reach the quickest?

Logically, one would presume that the knight would move much more quickly to d4 than to any of the other squares. Well, let's try each square in turn and see what happens.

a) The a8-square: The knight can reach this square in three moves, e.g. b2-a4-b6-a8.

b) The h1-square: Here the path is similar to 'a' and takes the same amount of time, e.g. b2-d1-f2-h1.

c) The h8-square: This square is further away and so it takes the knight a little longer. Nevertheless, it can achieve its goal with just four moves, e.g. b2-d3-e5-f7-h8.

d) The d4-square: Finally, let's try to get to this central square which appears to be just a hop away for the knight. Remarkably, it is not possible for the knight to reach this square in less than four moves! Try it and see.

TIP: The knight is a tricky piece!

Paradoxically it turns out that the a8- and h1-squares are more accessible to the knight than d4. Similarly it takes just as long for the knight to reach d4 as to reach h8!

The Pawn

The pawns are the foot soldiers or infantry of chess. They begin the game on the second row (for White this is the second rank, while for Black it is the seventh rank) and move forward along their respective files. They can only go forwards, pawns are not allowed to retrace their steps and move backwards. From their initial position pawns can move either one or two squares, but they are then restricted to a move of just one square. Thus in diagram 10, the white pawn on b2, being on its initial square, can move to either b3 or b4. The same option exists for the black pawn on d7 which can move either to d6 or d5. On the kingside the white pawn on f4 has already moved and thus only has f5 at its disposal. This pawn also blocks the advance of its colleague at f3 and this pawn thus has no possible moves at all. The black pawn at h7 has not yet moved but the 'two-square' option is unavailable as the white knight occupies h5.

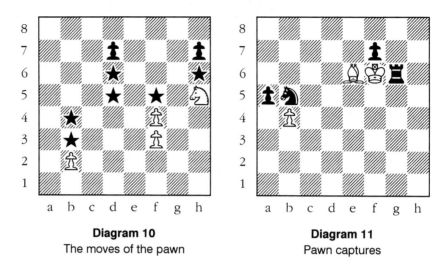

Diagram 10
The moves of the pawn

Diagram 11
Pawn captures

The pawns are unique among the chess forces in that their method of capture differs from the method by which they move. In diagram 11, one might expect that the white pawn on b4 would be able to capture the black knight on b5, but this is not the case. Pawns capture by moving one square forwards diagonally rather than along a file. Thus this pawn is able to capture the black pawn on a5 but not the black knight. Meanwhile, the black pawn on f7 can capture the white bishop on e6. In fact this is the only move available to this pawn as its advance is prevented by the white king.

 WARNING: Unlike all the pieces, pawns are not able to retrace their steps. Therefore you should always think carefully before advancing a pawn – you will never be able to return it to the square from which it came.

The King

The king is able to move one square in any direction, horizontally, vertically or diagonally. Thus in diagram 12 the black king can move to a7, b7 and b8. The white king has seven possible moves: six are indicated, while it is also possible for the white king to capture the black knight on f3. If White chose to play this move, the king would come to the f3-square and the black knight would be removed from the board. The e4-square is not available as this is occupied by a white pawn.

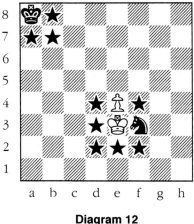

Diagram 12
The moves of the king

Check and Checkmate

The king is your most important piece (if not the most powerful) as the ultimate aim of the game is to capture the opposing king. When your king is threatened by an opposing piece this is known as 'check' and you *must* escape from the check with your very next move.

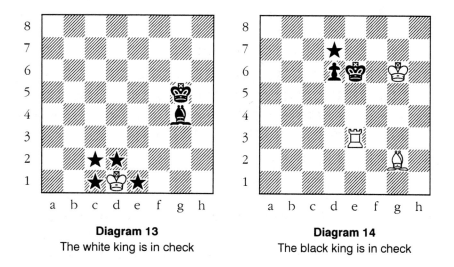

Diagram 13
The white king is in check

Diagram 14
The black king is in check

In diagram 13 the white king is threatened by the black bishop and so must escape from this threat. Fortunately there are four possible ways of doing this – by moving to c1, c2, d2 or e1. Note that White cannot move to e2 as the black bishop covers this square. By moving to e2 the white king would remain in check, which is not allowed.

In diagram 14, the black king is in check from the white rook and the situation is more precarious. Of the eight possible moves of the black king, seven are not possible: The king cannot go to f5, f6 or f7 as these squares are covered by the white king (note that the kings can never be side by side as they would both be in check). Additionally, e7 and e5 are unavailable as moving to either of these would not escape the check from the rook. Finally, d5 is covered by the white bishop and d6 is occupied by a black pawn. Fortunately for Black there is a safe move available – the king can move to d7.

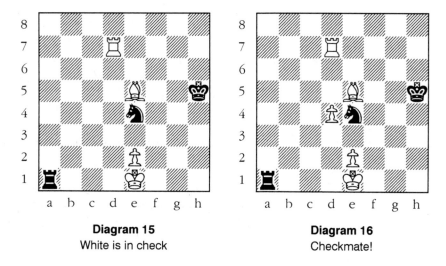

Diagram 15
White is in check

Diagram 16
Checkmate!

If you are in check, although you are obliged to deal with the threat to your king, moving the king is not the only option. There are two other ways to escape from the check:

a) Capture the attacking piece, thus removing the threat entirely.

b) Insert one of your own pieces into the line of fire, thus blocking the threat.

In diagram 15, White is in check, and has no possibility to move the king (can you see why?). However, the capturing and blocking options are both available. White can capture the black rook with the bishop, or block the check by interposing the rook on d1.

However, if we change the position slightly by adding a white pawn on d4 (diagram 16), the situation changes completely. White is in check and still cannot move the king, but the two saving moves with the rook and the bishop have both been disrupted by the addition of the pawn. White has no saving resource and has been checkmated! The game is over and Black wins.

TIP: Always keep an eye on possible checks both to your own king and to your opponent's. Although a check might not lead to checkmate, it always severely reduces your options.

Players learning the game sometimes try their luck in such a situation by saying 'Well, I can't deal with the threat to my king, but how about if I move my rook to h7, and threaten your king? Then if you capture my king, I will capture yours in reply.' If you thought of this – congratulations! You are a determined fighter and this attribute will serve you well in your games. However, here you are out of luck – checkmate concludes the game, end of story.

Piece Mobility

A key concept in chess is mobility – how free your pieces are to move around the board. An advantage in mobility can be very useful. It is worth taking a quick look at all the different pieces and considering how much their mobility is restricted by being placed away from the centre of the board.

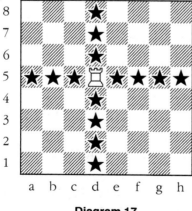

Diagram 17
The rook in the centre

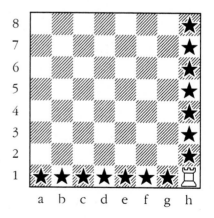

Diagram 18
The rook in the corner

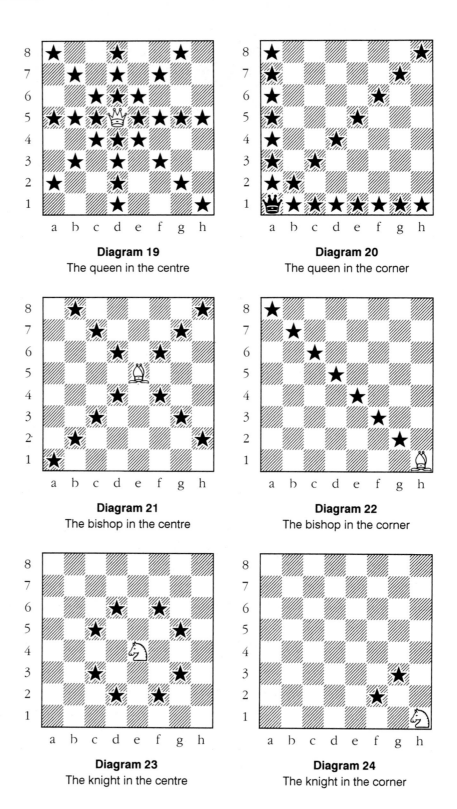

Diagram 19
The queen in the centre

Diagram 20
The queen in the corner

Diagram 21
The bishop in the centre

Diagram 22
The bishop in the corner

Diagram 23
The knight in the centre

Diagram 24
The knight in the corner

Consider the following table:

Piece	Central moves	Corner moves	Reduction in mobility
Rook	14	14	0%
Queen	27	21	22%
Bishop	13	7	46%
Knight	8	2	75%

From this we can see that the rook is not hampered at all by being away from the centre, whereas the queen remains very powerful even with a slightly reduced influence. However, the minor pieces are severely hampered by being located away from the central zone, particularly the knight.

The Mobility of the King

To conclude, we should also consider the mobility of the king. As we shall see, it is not always desirable to enhance the mobility of the king due to the possibilities of check and checkmate.

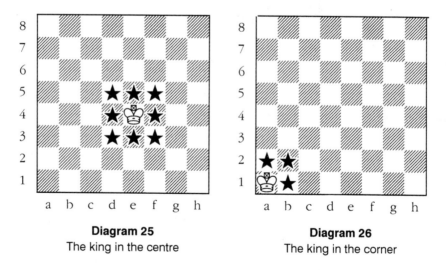

Diagram 25
The king in the centre

Diagram 26
The king in the corner

From diagrams 25 and 26 it is clear that the king loses a great deal of mobility by being stuck in the corner. The number of available moves is reduced from eight to three, equating to a loss in mobility of 63% – a figure which would place it between the bishop and knight in the above table. However, because the king is the most important piece (checkmate ends the game), a key component of chess strategy is to give it as much protection as possible. This often means that, early on in the game, the king will be tucked away and protected by pieces and pawns. In such circumstances it will have highly reduced mobility, but this is a tiny price to pay to give his majesty maximum protection.

However, all this can change as the position on the board simplifies. When material is reduced – especially when queens have been exchanged – the danger to the king becomes less and it can often become a powerful fighting unit in its own right. Nevertheless, early in the game, it should be well guarded.

Try it Yourself

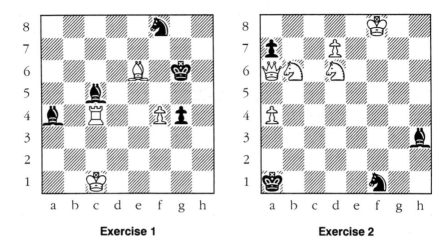

Exercise 1   Exercise 2

Exercise 1: Which moves and captures are available to:
a) The white rook? b) The black knight?

Exercise 2: Which moves and captures are available to:
a) The white queen? b) The black bishop?

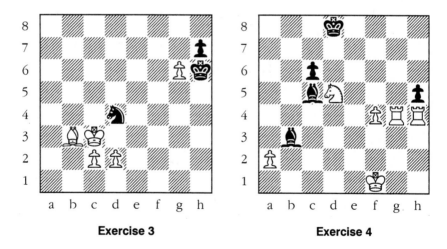

Exercise 3   Exercise 4

Exercise 3: Which of the two kings has more possible moves, including captures?

Exercise 4: What options are available to:
a) The white pawns on a2 and f4? b) The black pawns on c6 and h5?

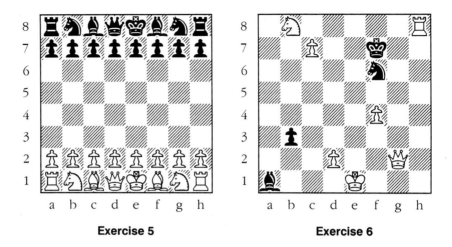

Exercise 5   Exercise 6

Exercise 5: This is the starting position for a chess game. How many possible moves does White have?

Exercise 6: As we know, the players move alternately in chess. However, for the sake of this puzzle, let us assume that White makes the next few moves without Black replying. How can White capture the black bishop on a1 with:
a) Two queen moves? b) Three rook moves?

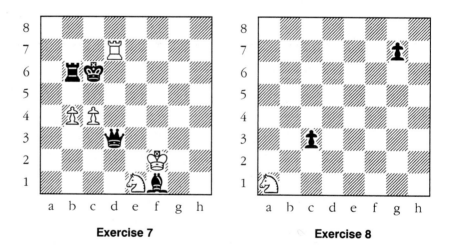

Exercise 7   Exercise 8

Exercise 7: Which of the two kings has more available moves?

Exercise 8: Which pawn can the white knight capture the quickest – the c3-pawn or the g7-pawn?

Summary

The queen, rook, bishop, knight and pawn all move in different ways. The queen is the most powerful piece and the pawn is the weakest.

If your king is threatened (in check), you must deal with this before doing anything else. If you cannot escape from check you have been checkmated!

All pieces, with the exception of the rook, have most mobility when placed in the centre of the board. The one most handicapped by being in the corner, or on the edge, is the knight.

Chapter Three

Notation and Unusual Moves

- ◼ **Algebraic Notation**
- ◼ **Castling**
- ◼ **Pawn Promotion**
- ◼ ***En Passant***
- ◼ **Try it Yourself**

Algebraic Notation

One of the most wonderful features of chess is the ability to record every game ever played. You can note down all the moves of a game as you are playing it and then recreate the battle later at your own leisure. This allows you to analyse the game, identify mistakes and seek out ways to improve your play. However, games are not always replayed for such instructional reasons. If you have played a beautiful game, perhaps winning with a clever combination, it is difficult to resist the temptation to play it over and over, admiring your brilliant achievement. Many players go one step further and show such games to all their friends in order that they might share in their delight.

Furthermore, there is a huge literature on chess and in order to access this wealth of material successfully all you need to be able to do is understand chess notation. Fortunately, the modern style – known as algebraic notation – is very straightforward and is now in more or less universal use.

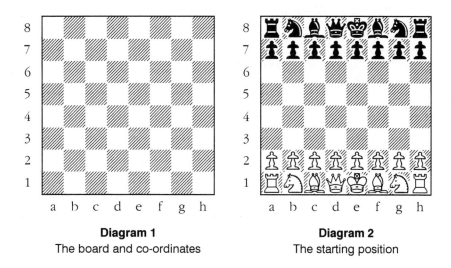

| **Diagram 1** | **Diagram 2** |
| The board and co-ordinates | The starting position |

Having looked at the previous material you should by now be familiar with the idea of the squares on the chessboard being referred to by co-ordinates (see diagram 1). The method by which a chess move is recorded is to give the symbol of the piece followed by the square to which the piece moves. When a pawn is moved, only the square on which the pawn arrives is given. First, a quick recap on the symbols used for the pieces:

Piece	Letter	Symbol
King	K	♔
Queen	Q	♕
Rook	R	♖
Bishop	B	♗
Knight	N	♘
Pawn	P	♙

Let us put this into practice, and see how we can write down the moves of a game, starting from the initial position (see diagram 2).

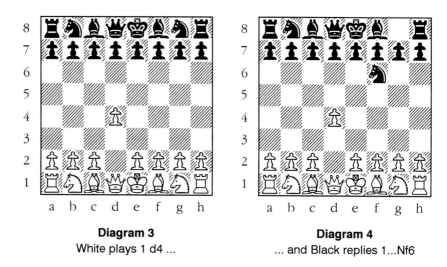

Diagram 3	Diagram 4
White plays 1 d4 ...	... and Black replies 1...Nf6

As we know, White moves first and, for the sake of this example, starts the game by playing the pawn from d2 to d4 (diagram 3). Black responds by moving the knight from g8 to f6 (diagram 4) – remember that knights can hop over intervening units. The 'score' of the moves would now be written as follows:

1 d4 Nf6

The '1' indicates that this is the first move of the game and, conventionally, White's move is always given first. (Remember that with a pawn move we do not need to indicate that it is a pawn that has moved. Although it would be quite logical to write 1 Pd4 for White's opening move this is not done as the 'P' is superfluous.)

Sometimes the situation arises where the first move of a given sequence is a black move – for example there may have been an annotation after the white move. In that case we indicate this by the addition of three dots. Thus Black's first move can be represented as 1...Nf6, indicating that the white move (in this case 1 d4) has already been played.

Let us now continue with the second move. White decides to move another pawn and so plays from c2 to c4. Black responds a further pawn move, but this time decides to advance just one square – from e7 to e6. We record this sequence as follows:

2 c4 e6

We now have the position given in diagram 5.

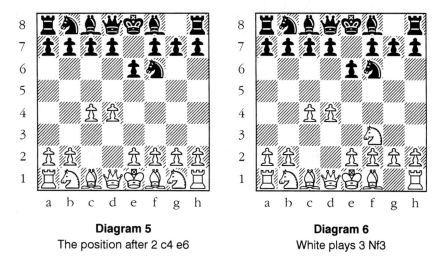

Diagram 5	**Diagram 6**
The position after 2 c4 e6	White plays 3 Nf3

White now brings out a piece, playing the knight on the king-side from g1 to f3 (see diagram 6).

NOTE: With piece moves (as opposed to pawn moves) we need to indicate which piece has moved as well as the square to which it has arrived.

3 Nf3

Black responds by developing the dark-squared bishop from f8 to b4 (diagram 7), also giving check to the white king. When a check is given we indicate this with the addition of a plus sign at the end of the move.

3...Bb4+

Perhaps Black is optimistically hoping that this is checkmate? Well, not quite. Although White cannot move the king (d2 does not escape from the check) and cannot capture the black bishop, there are several ways to interpose a piece and block the check. White chooses to use the knight and brings it out to c3 (diagram 8).

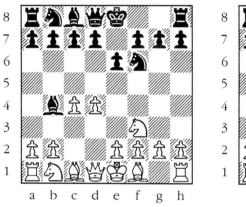

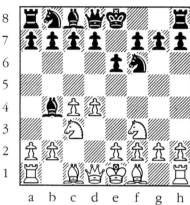

Diagram 7
Black checks with 3...Bb4+

Diagram 8
White blocks the check with 4 Nc3

4 Nc3

Black now decides to capture the white knight on c3 which, incidentally, will also give check. Captures are indicated by the addition of a 'x', placed between the piece symbol and the square. Thus:

4...Bxc3+ (see diagram 9)

White now recaptures this piece with the pawn on b2 – remember that pawns capture by moving one square diagonally. Normally when we write down a pawn move we only give the square on which the pawn arrives. However, when a capture is made we also give the file from which the pawn has moved and insert the 'x' as for the piece capture. In this case, the pawn has moved from the b-file and so we write:

5 bxc3

We are now well into the game which will continue with Black's fifth move from diagram 10.

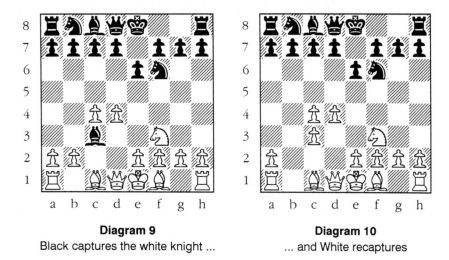

Diagram 9
Black captures the white knight ...

Diagram 10
... and White recaptures

More about Notation

Occasionally, a position arises where a little extra information is required to avoid any ambiguity. This occurs when it is possible for two similar pieces to make the same move. In that case some clarification is needed to identify which piece has actually made the move. Consider the position in diagram 11:

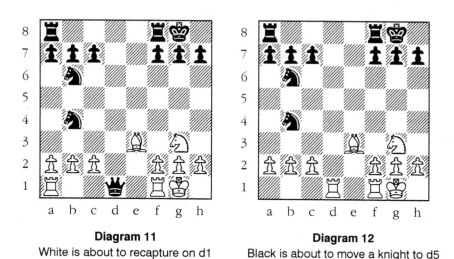

Diagram 11
White is about to recapture on d1

Diagram 12
Black is about to move a knight to d5

Black has just captured the white queen on d1 and White wants to reply by recapturing with the rook on a1. If we wrote this move down as 1 Rxd1, it would not be clear which rook White had used to take the white queen, as the other rook on f1 could also have performed this task. Therefore, we identify which rook has actually made the move by writing 1 Raxd1, indicating that the rook from the a-file has been used.

It is not always good enough to use a file to distinguish between two possible moves. Consider diagram 12, where White has just played 1 Raxd1. Black now decides to move the knight from b4 to d5, but we notice that the other knight, on b6, could also move to d5. However, writing 1...Nbd5 does not resolve the ambiguity, as both knights are on the b-file. The solution here is to use the rank to distinguish between the knights. Thus we write 1...N4d5 and everything is clear.

Annotation Symbols

Many theoretical works on chess use a completely languageless notation to describe the game. To the untutored eye, such texts can look like hieroglyphics with strange symbols denoting factors such as 'small advantage to White', 'Black is winning' or even 'space advantage and the two bishops'. However, the following special symbols, attached to individual moves, are much more common and can be seen in most books and chess columns in the general press. Such analytical marks are very useful and can help to clarify what has been happening during a game.

Symbol	Meaning
...	Black move follows
!	Good move
!!	Excellent move
?	Bad move
??	Blunder
!?	Interesting move
?!	Dubious move

Three Special Moves

There are three other moves which are possible in a chess game: castling, promotion and en passant captures. Let us look at each of these in turn.

Castling

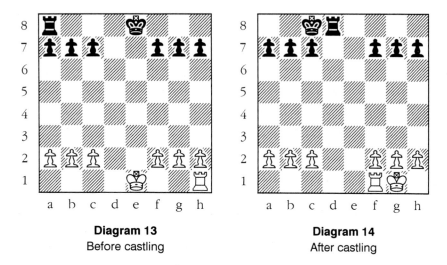

Diagram 13
Before castling

Diagram 14
After castling

During the course of the game it is possible to make a move known as 'castling', which can be played either on the queenside or kingside. When castling occurs, the king and rook move simultaneously along the back rank. The king always moves two squares and the rook hops over the king to land on the square beyond. Thus, in diagram 13, Black can castle on the queenside by moving the king from e8 to c8 and the rook from a8 to d8, while White can castle kingside by moving the king from e1 to g1 and the rook from h1 to f1. Diagram 14 shows the result of these moves.

Castling is often a useful move as it enables the king to become sheltered behind a row of pawns.

TIP: Castling is almost always a good move early on in the game as it brings the king to a safe position.

However, you cannot castle in every single circumstance. You are only allowed to make this move if the following conditions apply:

1. The king and rook must not have moved earlier on in the game.

2. The king must not be in check; nor must the king pass through check.

Thus in diagram 15, neither side is able to castle kingside: Black cannot do this as the king is in check from the white queen. White is also unable to castle kingside as, in order to do so, the king would have to pass through the f1-square, which is controlled by the black bishop. However, White would be able to castle queenside, by moving the king to c1 and the rook to d1. There is no impediment to this move.

Castling on the kingside, for either player, is written down as 0-0, while castling on the queenside is represented by 0-0-0.

Diagram 15
When castling is not permitted

Pawn Promotion

The pawn, as is obvious from its limited mobility, is much weaker than any of the pieces. However, an absolutely key element to the game of chess is the ability of a pawn to 'promote' by breaking through to the opponent's back rank. For White this means advancing all the way to the eighth rank, while for Black it would be the first rank. A pawn which does this is 'promoted' and can be replaced by a piece of your choice. In more than 99% of cases this will be a queen, as this is the most powerful piece. It is so common to choose a queen that promoting a pawn is often referred to as 'queening' a pawn.

An enterprising player might try to promote a pawn to a king, in order to have another monarch should the first one get checkmated. Unfortunately, this is not allowed. A pawn can only promote to a queen, rook, bishop or knight. Furthermore, when a pawn reaches the opponent's back rank, it must promote – you cannot simply leave it there as a pawn.

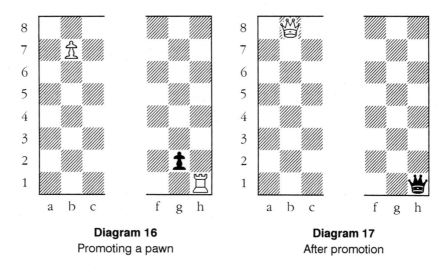

Diagram 16	**Diagram 17**
Promoting a pawn	After promotion

In diagram 16 the white pawn can advance from b7 to b8, when this pawn will be removed from the board and replaced with a white queen, rook, bishop or knight, according to the desire of the white player. Similarly, the black pawn on g2 can promote on g1 but could alternatively capture the white rook on h1, when it would also promote.

 NOTE: Pawn promotion is absolutely fundamental to chess. The ability of the pawn to dramatically increase its value by reaching the back row means that a small advantage of just one extra pawn can often decide a game.

Pawn promotion is written down by identifying the pawn move and then adding the symbol for the piece to which it has promoted. Thus from diagram 17, the two moves would be: 1 b8Q and 1...gxh1Q.

En Passant

The *en passant* (French for 'in passing') rule is probably the one that causes most confusion amongst beginners. It occurs when a pawn advances two squares on its initial move and finds itself adjacent to an opposing pawn. The opposing pawn then has the option to capture this pawn as if it had only moved one square. However, this capture can only take place immediately. If the player with the chance to make the *en passant* capture does something else instead, the chance is lost – you cannot come back and make the capture on a later move.

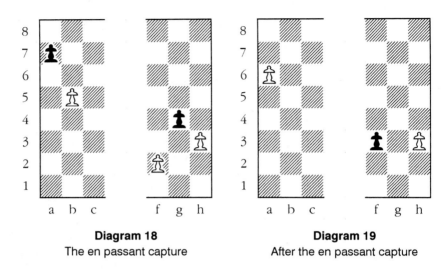

Diagram 18
The en passant capture

Diagram 19
After the en passant capture

In diagram 18 if Black advances the pawn from a7 to a5, White can respond by capturing this pawn as if it had only moved one square, i.e. from a7 to a6. Similarly, if the white pawn advances from f2 to f4, Black could take as if the pawn had only moved to f3. The en passant capture is only possible if the pawn moves from its initial square. Thus, if the white pawn on h3 moves to h4, the capture is not possible.

The *en passant* capture is written as if the pawn had only advanced one square and then been captured. Thus in diagram 19: on the kingside the sequence would be 1 f4 exf3, while on the queenside we would see 1...a5 2 bxa6.

The reason for this peculiar rule is that, originally, pawns were only allowed to advance one square from their initial position. However, this made chess a very slow game and so the two-step rule was introduced to speed things up a bit. However, it then seemed wrong that, for example, a white pawn which had advanced to e5 could be 'passed by' in one move by a pawn going from d7 to d5. Thus if this happens the white player has the option of capturing *en passant*.

The *en passant* rule is difficult and, paradoxically, the more familiar you become with the game, the harder it seems to integrate it into your knowledge of the rules. Many players achieve a quite reasonable standard without really understanding the move. I actually became a moderate strength club player with only a vague idea of how the rule worked.

I soon came unstuck in a club match where I was playing with the white pieces and achieved a favourable endgame. I cannot remember the exact position but an element of it was something akin to that shown in diagram 20.

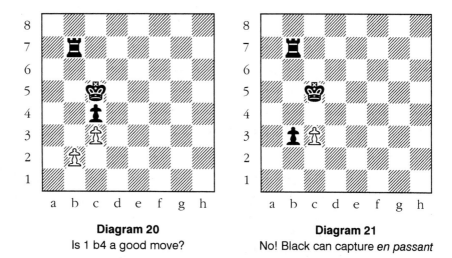

Diagram 20

Is 1 b4 a good move?

Diagram 21

No! Black can capture *en passant*

Here my opponent was pressing down against my pawn on b2 with the rook on the b-file. I was unsure what to do about this, as protecting the pawn was not an attractive option. However, I then had the brain wave of advancing the pawn two squares. This seemed wonderful. The pawn would be solidly protected by its colleague on c3 and would simultaneously give check to the black king. I played it without further thought.

My opponent thought for a few minutes and then, with a triumphant cry of '*en passant!*' removed my b-pawn from the board and placed his own c-pawn on b3 (see diagram 21). I was horrified. Not only had I lost a pawn but now my opponent had a powerful pawn on b3, rushing down to promote.

Not being *au fait* with this rule, I couldn't argue with what had happened (in fact his move was perfectly legitimate), but I was determined to get my own back. Never mind, I thought, at least I now know how this funny rule works. I managed to deal with this pawn and later we reached a position where the kingside structure was as shown on diagram 22.

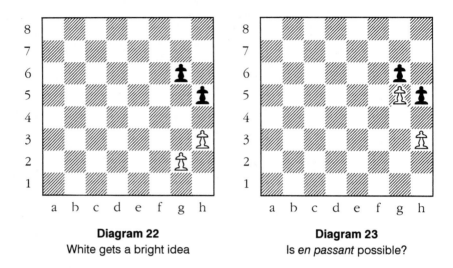

Diagram 22
White gets a bright idea

Diagram 23
Is *en passant* possible?

Here I had my second brain wave of the evening and advanced my pawn from g2 to g4. A move or two later, I advanced it again from g4-g5 (see diagram 23), and held my breath. My opponent fell for my 'trap' and did something on the queenside. With a euphoric cry of *'en passant!'* I removed his h-pawn from the board and placed my own g-pawn on h6.

Unfortunately, my 'triumph' was short-lived. His understanding of the rules was better than mine and he was having none of this. He patiently explained that I could only do this if his pawn had just moved from h7 to h5. I sheepishly retracted the move and played something else. I would strongly recommend that newcomers to the game learn the *en passant* rule properly so that they will be able to avoid such embarassing experiences.

Try it Yourself

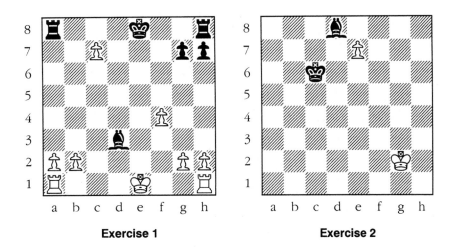

Exercise 1   **Exercise 2**

Exercise 1: Which castling moves are possible with
a) White to move? b) Black to move?

Exercise 2: White has three ways to promote the pawn whilst
also giving check. What are they? Bear in mind that it is not
essential to promote to a queen.

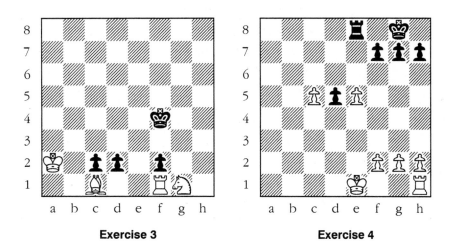

Exercise 3   **Exercise 4**

Exercise 3: Which pawns can Black promote, and on which
squares? Keep an eye on the position of the black king.

Exercise 4: Black has just advanced the d-pawn from d7 to d5.
Can White capture this pawn en passant and if so, how?

Summary

Castling is permitted as long as the king and rook have not previously moved, the king is not in check and the king is not moving through check.

Pawns reaching the opponent's back rank promote to a more valuable piece – nearly always the queen.

En passant gives a player the option of preventing an unmoved pawn from 'passing by' a pawn on the fifth rank.

Chapter Four

Winning and Drawing Games

- **Checkmate**

- **Stalemate**

- **Perpetual Check**

- **Drawing by Agreement**

- **Try it Yourself**

Checkmate

In chapter two we took a brief look at the concept of checkmate and there now follows a deeper examination. Checkmating themes are crucial because they recur again and again and a knowledge of the typical patterns that arise will help you both to formulate plans to checkmate your opponent as well as avoiding this fate yourself.

As we have already seen the king, in common with almost all the other pieces, is severely hampered by being in the corner or on the edge of the board. Remember that in order to checkmate the king it is necessary to remove all possible flight squares. Therefore the less of these there are – the better!

Back-Rank Checkmates

Probably the most common mating idea is with the major pieces along the back rank. Diagrams 1 and 2 show typical examples.

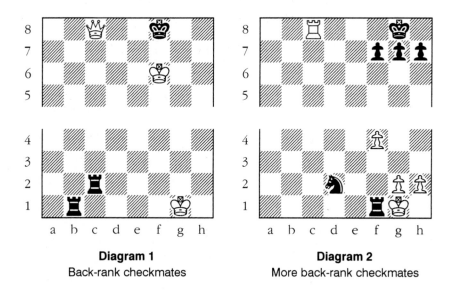

Diagram 1
Back-rank checkmates

Diagram 2
More back-rank checkmates

The upper half of diagram 1 shows a typical concluding position for giving checkmate with just a queen and a king. The white king takes away the flight squares e7, f7 and g7 while the white queen has the back row covered. In the lower half we see the power of a pair of rooks acting together. The rook on c2 takes the role of the white king in the previous example – denying the white king a chance to flee by escaping up the board. Meanwhile its colleague on b1 delivers the fatal back-row check.

One reason that back-row checkmates are so common is that players often castle their king at an early stage of the game. This is generally a good idea, as the king then has the protection of a wall of pawns in front of it which helps to thwart direct attacks. However, the barrier formed by these pawns also prevents the king from escaping up the board. When this situation arises we speak of a player having a 'weak back rank'.

WARNING: Castling is nearly always a good idea, but it can expose the king to back-rank checkmates.

Typical methods of exploiting this are seen in diagram 2. In the upper half we see a simple mate by the white rook. In the lower half White has slightly freed the king by advancing the f-pawn but in this particular case it doesn't help. The black rook, which is delivering the fatal check along the back rank, also controls the f2-square, while an attempt to capture the black rook is thwarted by the knight on d2.

More Common Mating Themes

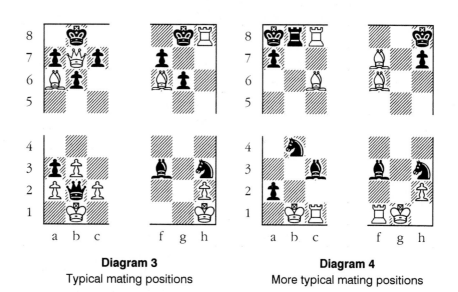

Diagram 3
Typical mating positions

Diagram 4
More typical mating positions

In diagrams 3 and 4, we see eight further examples of how the constriction of the king, either in the corner or on the back row, can lead to checkmating possibilities. In particular these positions show the power of the bishop working on the long diagonal (i.e. a1-h8 or h1-a8).

Resigning

It is not unusual (in fact it is extremely common) for a game to be terminated before checkmate has arisen. When defeat becomes inevitable a player will usually 'resign' the game and concede defeat without waiting to see how the opponent will actually deliver checkmate.

Drawing the Game

Not all chess games end in victory for one side – draws are perfectly possible. Although in the hurly-burly of club and social chess almost all games conclude decisively, at the highest levels a draw is the most common outcome. There are various ways in which the game can be drawn:

a) Stalemate

b) Perpetual check

c) By mutual agreement.

Let us consider each of these in turn.

Stalemate

Stalemate arises when a player, whose turn it is to play, has no legal move. Unlike draughts (checkers) where this results in a win for the opponent, stalemate in chess results in a draw. Stalemate most commonly occurs in very simple endgames and is critical in determining the outcome of positions with much reduced material.

Consider the positions in diagram 5. In the upper two examples Black, whose turn it is to play, has no legal move and is in stalemate. The example on the left is a very common theme. White, playing with king and pawn against king, is attempting to promote this pawn to a queen. It would then be possible to win the game, as king and queen can give checkmate. Unfortunately, Black has blocked the path of this pawn and has no possible moves and the white king and pawn control the five squares immediately around the black king.

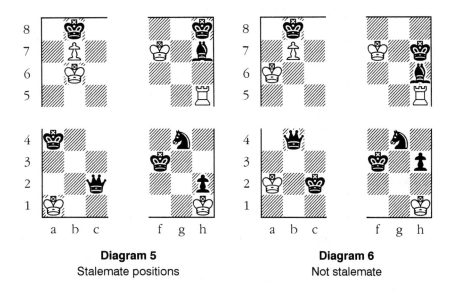

Diagram 5
Stalemate positions

Diagram 6
Not stalemate

The remaining three examples in diagram 5 all show situations where the side with material superiority is attempting to win but has been scuppered by a stalemate defence. They are all typical endgame positions. In the top right diagram it is Black to play, while in the lower two diagrams it is White's move.

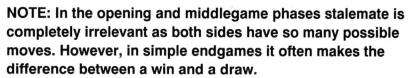

NOTE: In the opening and middlegame phases stalemate is completely irrelevant as both sides have so many possible moves. However, in simple endgames it often makes the difference between a win and a draw.

Not Stalemate

In diagram 6 the previous four examples have been slightly altered. The positions are no longer stalemate and, in fact, the side with the superior force will win immediately:

Top left: 1...Kc7 2 Ka7 and White will promote the pawn and win.

Top right: 1...Kh8 2 Rxh6 checkmate.

Bottom left: 1 Ka1 is White's one and only move. Black now has a choice of checkmating moves: 1...Qa3, 1...Qa4, 1...Qa5, 1...Qb1 and 1...Qb2 all deliver the fatal blow.

Bottom right: 1 Kg1 Kg3 2 Kh1 Nf2+ 3 Kg1 h2+ 4 Kf1 (note that the black knight now prevents the white king from returning to the corner) 4...h1Q+ and Black will quickly force checkmate with his material advantage.

Perpetual Check

Consider the position in diagram 7, where it is White to play. On the queenside Black has succeeded in setting up one of the typical checkmating combinations that we saw earlier. The threat is 1...Qb2 mate and, even though it is White's turn to play, there is nothing to be done to prevent this. The queen and rook cannot do anything to defend and White's king has no possibility to escape. So, White tries the only chance to continue the game and plays...

1 Qg6+

...giving check with the queen. As we know, you must always escape from check, even when you can give checkmate yourself with one move. Therefore Black replies with the only legal move

1...Kh8

And we arrive at the position in diagram 8.

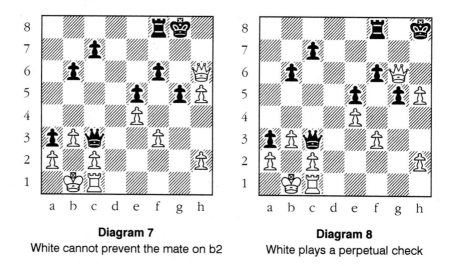

Diagram 7
White cannot prevent the mate on b2

Diagram 8
White plays a perpetual check

At first sight this does not seem to have helped White. The queen still cannot return to defend and Black's impending checkmate seems unstoppable. However, White has another check...

2 Qh6+

to which Black's only reply is

2...Kg8

Note that we have now returned to the original position and White can repeat the manoeuvre with

3 Qg6+ Kh8 4 Qh6+ Kg8

and can continue to give checks ad infinitum. Although Black has a crushing threat, there is no way to escape from White's checking sequence and the game is drawn by perpetual check.

Perpetual check often occurs when one side launches an attack but does not quite have sufficient initiative to land a checkmate or win material. The position in diagram 9 arose in a game played between the current world champion, Garry Kasparov, and the man he defeated, previous world champion Anatoly Karpov. It was played in the 11th game of their World Championship match from 1990, held in New York and Lyons.

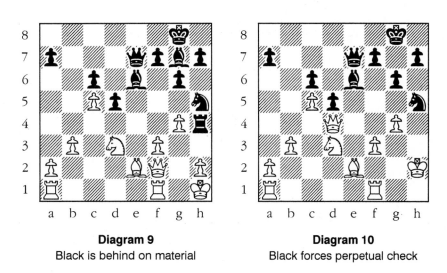

Diagram 9
Black is behind on material

Diagram 10
Black forces perpetual check

Kasparov, playing Black, has launched a kingside attack but is down on material, having only a bishop against White's rook. However, he now sacrificed even more material:

1...Bd4!

The black bishop attacks the white queen.

2 Qxd4

White is not obligated to capture this bishop but Karpov, having studied the position at some length, decided that he had no better alternative.

2...Rxh2+! 3 Kxh2 (see diagram 10)

Black is now two rooks down, but has everything under control.

3...Qh4+ 4 Kg2 Qg3+ 5 Kh1 Qh3+

and Black has set up the same perpetual check that we saw in the previous example.

Drawing by Agreement

By far the most common way for a game to be drawn is by the mutual agreement of the players. Usually, after a hard fight (or sometimes not so hard), a position arises where both players realise that there is no realistic hope of making progress and that neither will ever win the game. They may then agree to call the game a draw.

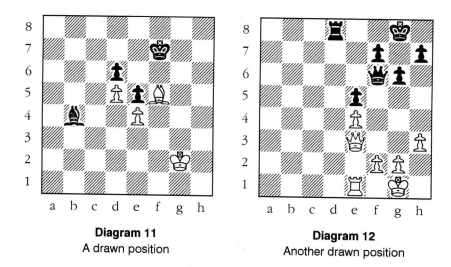

Diagram 11	Diagram 12
A drawn position	Another drawn position

In diagram 11, material is equal and the players have what is known as 'opposite-coloured bishops'. This is not said for the simple reason that one is black and one is white, it means that the white bishop operates on the light squares, whereas the black bishop operates on the dark squares. Opposite-coloured bishops lead to notoriously drawish positions as these two pieces can never interact. In this particular case, neither side has a point of weakness and although both players can continue to shuffle around, it is obvious that nothing of importance will ever happen. The best thing to do is to agree to a draw.

In diagram 12, material is again equal, although here there is much more of a chance that something will happen. However, if one side tried to attack the other it is likely that they would leave themselves exposed and that their attack would backfire. This is another typical situation where a draw might be agreed.

The position does not have to be level for a draw to be agreed. Psychology can often play a part. For example, if a player gets into a good position against a much stronger opponent, it can be a clever ploy to offer a draw. The opponent is now in a difficult situation. Being the stronger player, he would really expect to win the game. However, he has a bad position and it may be better to cut and run by accepting the draw rather than playing on and risking defeat.

However, do not always be too ready to agree to a draw, especially when you are still learning the game. It is important to develop a feel for the game and this can only come about through experience of playing many types of different position and seeing what happens. You will have plenty of time to agree draws later on in your career. If you have a good position against a good player, you can learn a great deal from trying to win the game. If they do manage to turn the position round and beat you, you can console yourself with the fact that it is a good learning experience (however, it does not necessarily feel like that at the time!).

 TIP: If you think you are doing badly and your opponent offers a draw do not be too quick to accept. They may just have made a horrible blunder and be trying to bale out before you spot it!

Try it Yourself

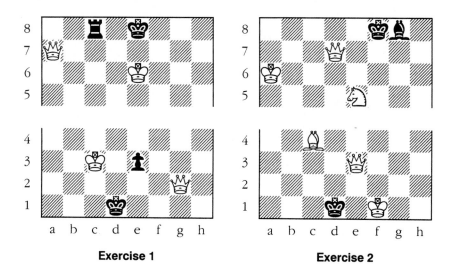

Exercise 1

Exercise 2

Exercises 1 and 2 In the above four diagrams, White can checkmate in one move. Can you see how?

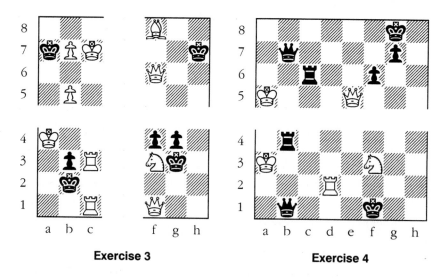

Exercise 3

Exercise 4

Exercise 3: In all four positions, Black is to play. Which positions are stalemate and which are not?

Exercise 4: In these two positions, White is to play, but he is badly behind on material in both cases. How can he save the day?

Summary

The most common mating theme is the back-rank checkmate. Always keep an eye out for this during your games.

It is important to understand how stalemate works – although irrelevant in openings and middlegames, it becomes crucial in the endgame.

If nothing is happening in the position and both you and your opponent are shuffling around aimlessly, you can always suggest that the game should be agreed a draw.

Chapter Five

It's a Material World

- ■ The Value of the Pieces
- ■ Two Important Questions
- ■ Guarding your Assets
- ■ Try it Yourself

The Value of the Pieces

As we already know, the ultimate aim in the game of chess is to checkmate the opponent's king, while avoiding the same fate befalling our own. However, although capturing the king is the eventual goal, it is not our first priority when starting a game. The opponent's king is usually far too well protected early on in the game for any direct attack to have much chance of success. The way in which most games are won is when one side makes a gain in material, with this advantage being slowly nursed to victory. This gain can be quite modest and even the acquisition of an extra pawn can be enough to assure eventual victory.

Why do we need Extra Material?

Hopefully, this should be obvious. If you are a general conducting a battle, would you rather have ten units against the opponent's five, or vice versa? Of course, quantity does not always imply quality. As we have already seen, some pieces have more mobility than others and this makes them more powerful. When you are involved in exchanges of pieces during your games, make sure that the units you are capturing are more valuable than the ones you are losing.

How Valuable are the Pieces?

Books on astronomy often describe the size of other planets in the solar system in terms of the earth. For example, the mass of the gigantic planet Jupiter is 318 times that of earth, while the much smaller Mercury has a mass just 0.055 times that of earth. We can perform a similar exercise with the chess pieces, using the pawn as the basic unit.

Piece	Value in terms of pawns
King	Not relevant
Queen	9
Rook	5
Bishop	3
Knight	3
Pawn	1

The above table is a very good guide to how you should rank

the pieces. The value of the king is not relevant. As this piece is never exchanged it has no 'trading' value. From this table, we can establish certain useful rules of thumb:

a) Bishops and knights (the minor pieces) are about equal.
b) A minor piece is worth three pawns.
c) A rook is worth a minor piece plus two pawns.
d) Two rooks are slightly better than a queen.
e) A queen is worth approximately a rook, plus a minor piece and a pawn.

TIP: The table of values is very important. Committing it to memory does not take long and will prove to be crucial when you are trying to work out what to do at the board.

This gives an indication as to which exchanges you should be looking to make and which you should avoid. Of course, it is important to bear in mind that this table is just a guide. The relative values of the pieces all fluctuate during the course of the struggle and strong players will make unconcious mental adjustments for this.

Let us see how this table can be used in practice (see diagram 1). Here White has various opportunities to capture material, some better than others. They are: 1 Bxb6, 1 Qxa8, 1 Qxf6 and 1 Rxd7. Let us consider each in turn:

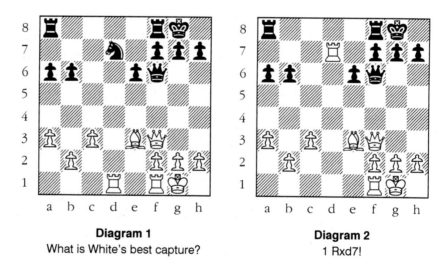

Diagram 1
What is White's best capture?

Diagram 2
1 Rxd7!

a) **1 Bxb6?** White captures a pawn but this turns out to be a bad deal. Black replies **1...Nxb6** and White has lost a bishop for a pawn.

b) **1 Qxa8?** This is even worse. The rook is defended by its partner on f8 and after **1...Rxa8** White has lost a queen for a rook.

c) **1 Qxf6**. This is fine, but unexciting. The black queen is protected and the reply will be **1...Nxf6**. The queens have been exchanged. This is an improvement on 'a' and 'b' as White hasn't lost anything – but he hasn't won anything either.

d) **1 Rxd7!** (see diagram 2). This is the way to go. Black's knight was unprotected and White has taken full advantage, netting a clear piece at no cost and leaving the balance sheet looking very healthy indeed. Note that Black can now capture the white queen with **1...Qxf3**, but White immediately recaptures with **2 gxf3** and retains the extra piece.

Two Important Questions

An understanding of how the pieces interact is absolutely fundamental to mastering chess. When playing your first few games there are two main questions you should ask yourself when your opponent has played and it is your move:

1. 'Is my opponent threatening any of my pieces?'
2. 'Can I make any favourable captures myself?'

The only way to ensure that you do not make any bad blunders yourself and that you spot any that your opponent makes, is to work through 'a' and 'b' when it is your move. This might seem to be a very laborious procedure, but you will not have to do it for very long. After a while it becomes instinctive. As your brain familiarises itself with the common patterns and sequences that arise during a game, you will automatically spot threats without having to look for them in such a painstakingly mechanical fashion.

NOTE: Checking the position before each move is not as tedious as it might appear. The position does not change drastically from one move to the next and so 90% of what you worked out on the last move will probably still apply.

It is rather like learning to drive. For a learner driver a simple task such as changing gear can seem immensely difficult.

There are so many things to remember: ease off the accelerator, depress the clutch, select a gear, change gear, release the clutch, hand back on the steering wheel and so on. And all the while you have to worry about the other elements that go with driving a car: steering, looking in front of you, checking the rear-view mirror, etc etc. A total nightmare. Put like this it is a wonder anybody ever learns to drive. However, as with all repetitive tasks, after a while control of the car becomes easier and, eventually, it becomes second nature and you no longer need to give it your conscious attention. Of course, such (over)confidence can also bring its own dangers – but that is another issue.

The same principle applies with learning to play chess. Unless you can conduct a lengthy series of moves without leaving your pieces *en prise*, you will forever be stuck in first gear and will constantly stall. However, do not despair. If you can approach each position in your games by asking yourself the above two questions, you will very quickly get a feel for how the pieces interact, what your opponent is threatening and what you can threaten yourself.

NOTE: *En prise* **is a chess term used to describe a piece which is left unprotected and vulnerable to capture.**

Let's look at another position (see diagram 3), and articulate the thought processes we need to go through.

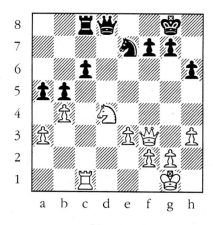

Diagram 3
Can White make a good capture?

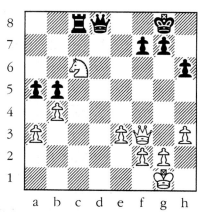

Diagram 4
White has lost rook for knight

You are playing White and it is your move. So:

a) 'Is my opponent threatening any of my pieces?'

Well, he is threatening two possible captures: 1...Qxd4 and 1...axb4. Are they serious? No. 1...Qxd4 is a disaster for Black as our knight is protected and he will lose his queen after 2 exd4. 1...axb4 captures a pawn, but we can recapture with 2 axb4 and maintain the balance.

b) 'Can I make any favourable captures myself?'

I could try 1 Qxf7+ but that is a waste of time as I lose my queen after 1...Kxf7. 1 Nxb5 is also possible, but this pawn is protected (by the c-pawn) so that is no good either. However, I have three possible ways to capture the c-pawn, 1 Qxc6, 1 Rxc6 and 1 Nxc6. Do any of these work?

1 Qxc6? loses the queen after either 1...Nxc6 or 1...Rxc6. 1 Rxc6?! is preferable but after 1...Nxc6 2 Nxc6 (see diagram 4) White has taken a knight and a pawn (four units) but lost a rook (five units) – not good business. Note that after this sequence, 1 Rxc6 Nxc6 2 Nxc6, Black will not play 2...Rxc6 3 Qxc6 as this would return the favour. Instead he will move his threatened queen, perhaps with 2...Qd6. However, **1 Nxc6!** (see diagram 5) works for White. Black can capture on this square twice, but White always has a safe recapture, i.e. **1...Nxc6 2 Rxc6 Rxc6 3 Qxc6** (see diagram 6) and White emerges with a safe extra pawn.

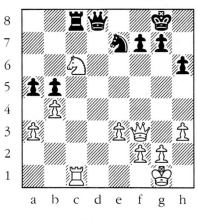

Diagram 5
1 Nxc6

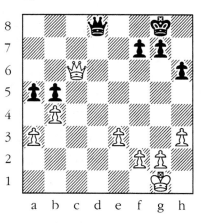

Diagram 6
White has emerged a pawn ahead

We could go on like this indefintely but the best way to gain this feeling is to practice yourself by playing games. Alternatively, play through games by very strong players. They will almost never make really bad blunders. So, if they have the opportunity to make favourable looking captures and turn them down, there is usually a good reason for it. See if you can work out what it is.

Guarding your Assets

It is good to keep an eye out for chances to capture your opponent's material, but what about when your pieces are attacked? What is the best way to deal with threats to your own forces?

In the same way that there are various methods of dealing with a check, there are various options for countering threats to your pieces. They are:

a) Move the piece away.
b) Defend the piece under attack.
c) Capture the piece that is making the threat.
d) Block the line of attack or, if all else fails...
e) Create such confusion elsewhere on the board that your opponent is distracted from carrying out his threat.

We will consider each in turn.

Move the Piece away

This is a very simple and effective response. In the film *Monty Python and the Holy Grail* King Arthur, when faced with perilous situations, would give the order to 'Run away' – and it is not a bad strategy. Two simple examples will suffice.

A common opening sequence is **1 e4 c6** This is known as the Caro-Kann Defence. **2 d4 d5 3 Nc3 dxe4 4 Nxe4**. Now Black can threaten the white knight with **4...Bf5** (see diagram 7). White drops the knight back with **5 Ng3**, returning the favour by attacking the black bishop, and the bishop also retreats with **5...Bg6**.

Players are often concerned that they may lose time if they are continually reacting to threats by moving away with their pieces. This can happen, but it is also possible that the player

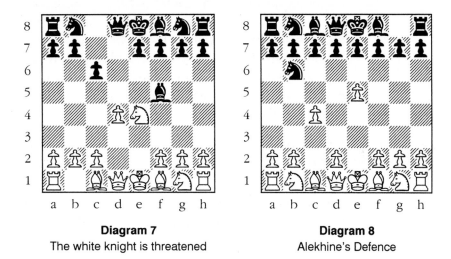

Diagram 7
The white knight is threatened

Diagram 8
Alekhine's Defence

doing the chasing is not necessarily furthering his aims. Consider the following opening, known as Alekhine's Defence. **1 e4 Nf6 2 e5 Nd5 3 c4 Nb6** (see diagram 8). Black seems to have achieved nothing while White has been advancing his pawns. In fact he can continue to kick the knight around even more with **4 c5 Nd5 5 Bc4** if he so wishes. However, this opening is perfectly respectable for Black, who is hoping that White will over-extend his position and leave himself open to a counterattack later on.

WARNING: Attacking the opponent's pieces always feels good – it gives us the impression that we are forcing the pace. However, do not create threats just for the sake of it. If the threats can be dealt with easily, you may just be weakening your position.

Defend the Piece under attack

If you have a piece which is well placed, you may be loath to move it away. In this case, defending it may be a good option. However, this possibility is (usually) only available if your piece is of less or equal value to the one threatening it. If your opponent attacks your queen with a bishop, there is not much point defending it – he will take it anyway as it is a much more valuable piece.

In diagram 9 we see a position from the 11th game of the World Championship match between Kasparov and Karpov, played in Moscow in 1985. Karpov, as Black, has just played his rook to d8, attacking the white bishop on d5. The bishop is on a strong central location, creating pressure on both sides of the board. Kasparov was thus loathe to move it away or exchange it for the less active black knight on c6. He therefore chose to defend it with **1 Rcd1**.

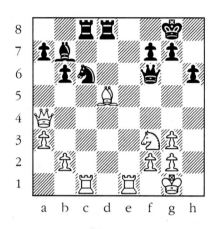

Diagram 9	**Diagram 10**
White has a strong bishop on d5	How should White defend the knight?

Although Kasparov's Rcd1 was a strong move it is often uneconomical for a piece as powerful as a rook to be reduced to defending a mere bishop. A far better way to protect a well placed piece is with a lowly pawn. In diagram 9 Kasparov did not have this option, but in our next example (see diagram 10) this proves to be a good plan.

Black is threatening the white knight on d5. It is beautifully placed in the centre of the board, so White does not want to move it. He could defend it with a rook, but his rooks are doing a good job creating pressure on the e-file and it would be a shame to move them away. The solution is **1 c4!**, anchoring the knight in place. Note that Black will never be able to remove this knight cheaply. His only remaining minor piece is a dark-squared bishop which can never threaten to exchange off the white knight. Black can rid the board of the troublesome knight with a rook but, as we know, that is an expensive trade to make.

TIP: In general it helps if your pawns protect your pieces rather than vice versa.

Capture the Piece making the Threat

If you can do this, and not enter into an unfavourable trade whilst doing so, this is usually a good idea. After the opening sequence **1 e4 e5 2 Nf3 Nc6 3 Bb5**. This is called the Ruy Lopez and is one of the oldest and most popular openings; Black's next move constitutes an unusual variation known as Bird's Defence. **3...Nd4**, White finds his bishop under threat from the black knight (see diagram 11). He could move it, or even defend it, but the best move is probably the simple **4 Nxd4**, removing the attacking piece.

Diagram 11

Black attacks the white bishop

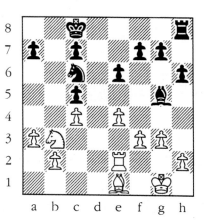

Diagram 12

Black's pawn on c5 is vulnerable

Sometimes it is possible to obligate your opponent to make a capture that helps to improve your position. In diagram 12, Black has a problem to solve. White is threatening the black pawn on c5. Black could defend the pawn with 1...Be7, but this is only a short-term solution. White would step up the pressure with 2 Bf2 and suddenly Black has no way to defend this pawn.

A more dynamic idea for Black is to play **1...Nd4!**, attacking the white rook and knight. White's only decent reply is to capture this knight with **2 Nxd4**, but now with **2...cxd4** Black has engineered a favourable alteration of the structure. The troublesome weak pawn on c5 has been eliminated and replaced with a strong central pawn on d4 which can, if necessary, easily be protected by ...Rd8 and/or ...c7-c5.

Block the Line of attack

This is a useful device to use in the opening, especially for an attack against the queen. For example, after **1 d4 e6 2 Nf3 b6**, White might to try his luck with **3 Bg5**, attacking the black queen (see diagram 13). Previously tried methods all fail: the queen cannot move away (all available squares are controlled by the white bishop); there is no point defending the queen (the bishop will take it anyway); and the only way to capture the attacking piece is with 3...Qxg5, but the white knight will then whip off the black queen.

The solution is to put something in the way. There are four ways of doing this: **3...Be7**, **3...Ne7**, **3...Nf6** and **3...f6**, and they are all perfectly good.

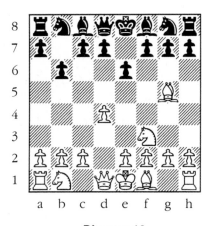

Diagram 13
The black queen is threatened

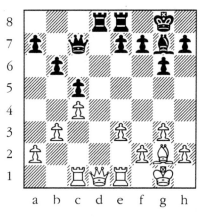

Diagram 14
Should White block the attack?

However, blocking an attack is a device which should be used with caution. In diagram 14 Black has just brought a rook to the d-file and threatened the white queen. It might seem like a good idea to interpose the bishop with **1 Bd5**. This blocks the threat and places the bishop on a useful central square. However, the bishop is now *pinned* (we shall examine the concept of the pin in more detail in the next chapter) against the queen and is unable to move. Black can exploit this with **1...e6**, when the white bishop is attacked and will be lost.

Create Confusion Elsewhere

This is a common ploy in politics and is well understood by spin doctors. Governments can often divert attention from an uncomfortable issue by 'manufacturing' good news elsewhere. This idea of rustling something up is also a good final try in chess when nothing else seems to work. The most powerful threat that you can generate is a check – a check always has to be dealt with immediately – and this can often provide the breathing space needed to get your position in order.

In diagram 15, White is threatening the black rook on f8 with the bishop on a3, and none of the usual methods to counter the attack work (can you see why?). Black's main problem is that the rook is hemmed in by its own pieces and cannot flee from the attack from the bishop. However, there is a solution. Black creates some space with **1...Qc6+!** and after, for example, **2 Kg1** can safely move the rook along the back rank to, say, c8.

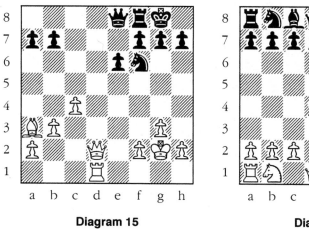

Diagram 15
Black's rook is stuck

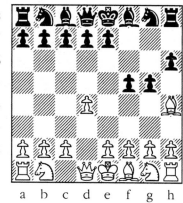

Diagram 16
Will the white bishop be trapped?

The opening sequence **1 d4 f5** is known as the Dutch Defence. After **2 Bg5 h6 3 Bh4 g5** (see diagram 16) everything seems to have gone wrong for White. The bishop on h4 is under attack and the only retreat square is g3. However, 4 Bg3 is met by 4...f4 when the bishop is trapped and White will lose a piece.

Unlike the previous example, White cannot even give a check here, but he can save himself with the calm **4 e3!** (see diagram 17). This sneaky move threatens Qh5 checkmate and means

Black has no time to capture the bishop.

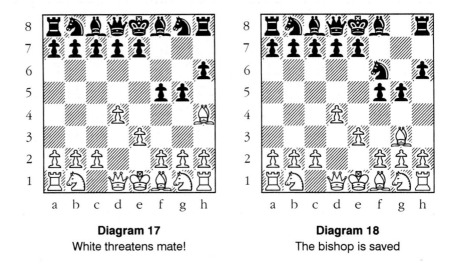

Diagram 17
White threatens mate!

Diagram 18
The bishop is saved

Black's best is now **4...Nf6**, developing the knight and covering h5 to prevent the checkmate. Now, however, White can retreat the bishop with **5 Bg3** (see diagram 18). That pawn on e3 now makes all the difference as this pawn covers the f4-square and **5...f4** can be met by **6 exf4 gxf4 7 Bxf4**.

Try it Yourself

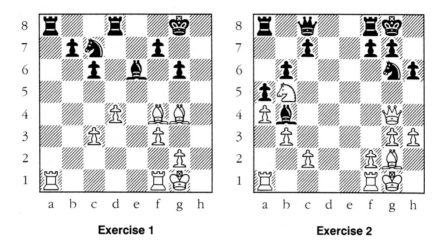

Exercise 1   **Exercise 2**

Exercises 1 and 2: White has various possible captures available. Find them all and identify which one is the best.

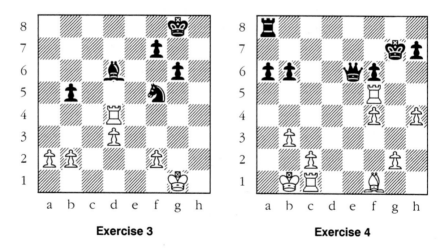

Exercise 3   **Exercise 4**

Exercises 3: Here White has a rook under attack on d4. Identify the safe squares for this piece to move to.

Exercise 4: What are White's options for dealing with the threat to the rook on f5?

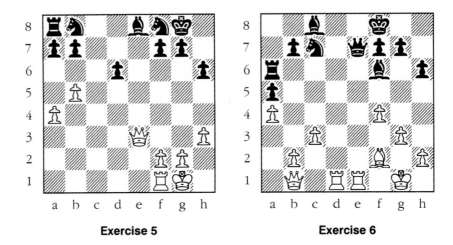

Exercise 5   **Exercise 6**

Exercise 5: The black bishop is attacked by the white queen. Black has various ways to deal with this threat. What are they?

Exercise 6: The black queen is under attack. How can Black combat this threat most effectively?

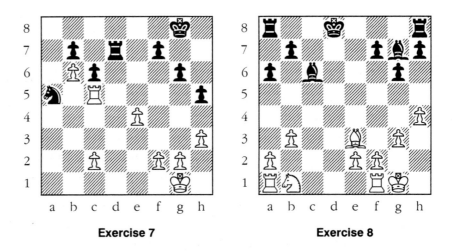

Exercise 7   **Exercise 8**

Exercise 7: Although Black is a piece up, the threat to the knight on a5 is awkward to meet. How can Black avoid having to return the extra material?

Exercise 8: The black bishop on g7 has the white rook on a1 in its sights. What is White's best defence?

Summary

Commit the table of piece values to memory. It is essential to know these values instinctively.

When it is your move, ask yourself the two key questions: 'Is my opponent threatening any of my pieces?' and 'Can I make any favourable captures myself?'

When one of your own pieces is threatened, the instinctive response is to move it away. However, this might not be best. See if you can use a different method of countering the attack.

Chapter Six

Introducing Tactics

- The Fork
- The Pin
- The Skewer
- Countering Tactical Threats
- Try it Yourself

When you have developed a feel for the interaction between the pieces, as described in the previous chapter, you will probably be able to overcome complete beginners by simply capturing the pieces they leave *en prise*, whilst avoiding leaving pieces unprotected yourself. However, when you come up against more experienced players you will find that they are far less obliging. They will be thinking along the same lines as you and may well prove remarkably reluctant to give away all their pieces at the earliest opportunity. When this happens you need to add a further dimension to your play – you need to develop your tactical skill. Good tactical vision will enable you to set traps for your opponent and to avoid falling for traps yourself.

Although tactical play can be very complex, there are three basic tactical ploys which act as the building blocks for more complex ideas. These are the fork, the pin and the skewer, and we shall look at each in turn.

The Fork

Probably the most basic and most easily understood of all chess tactics is the fork. A fork occurs when two threats are made simultaneously. A player can only make one move at a time and if there is no possibility to defend against both threats at the same time then one of these threats can be carried out on the next move. Usually these threats involve the capture of material. Let us consider some examples:

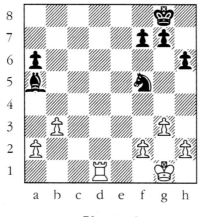

Diagram 1
Material is equal

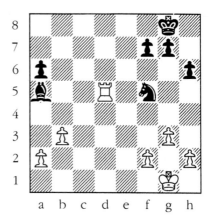

Diagram 2
The rook forks the bishop and knight

Diagram 1: At the moment, the material situation is balanced. White has a rook and a pawn (six units) against two minor pieces (also six units). However, after **1 Rd5!** (see diagram 2) White threatens both the black knight and bishop and, although Black can save one piece, he cannot save both. White will therefore win a piece and should then win the game easily.

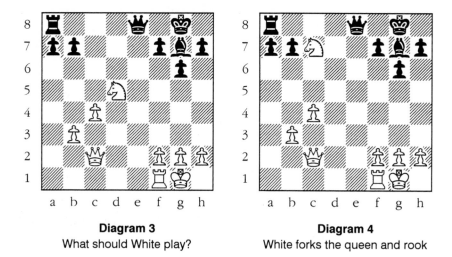

Diagram 3
What should White play?

Diagram 4
White forks the queen and rook

Diagram 3: Again material is equal with White having a knight against Black's bishop. However, White can now continue **1 Nc7!**, forking the black queen and rook. Both the black pieces (nine units and five units respectively) are more valuable than the white knight (three units) and so White will make a material gain. Of course, Black will elect to save the higher-valued queen – perhaps by playing 1...Qf8 – but after 2 Nxa8 Qxa8 White has made a substantial material gain which should be enough to win the game.

The importance of getting the king to safety early in the game has already been emphasised. While it remains in the open it can make a player highly vulnerable to a quick tactical knock-out, as the following example indicates. The position in diagram 5 arises after the opening moves **1 e4 c5 2 Nf3 d6 3 c3 Nf6 4 Be2**.

At first sight it looks as if White has allowed Black to capture an important central pawn. Why can't Black take the white e-pawn with his knight? The answer is that White has a queen fork planned and will meet the incautious **4...Nxe4?** with **5**

Qa4+! (see diagram 6). Black must deal with the check to his king and, although he has many ways of doing this, none of them will save the knight on e4.

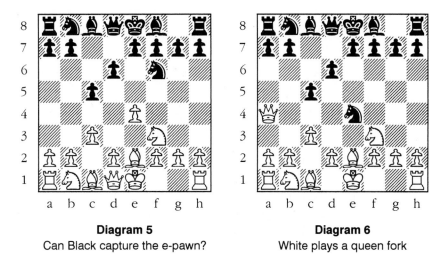

Diagram 5
Can Black capture the e-pawn?

Diagram 6
White plays a queen fork

TIP: A king in the centre often provides good opportunities for tactical tricks.

The queen is particularly good at forking pieces as it has such a powerful range of movement. Witness the following example, which occurred in the game Christiansen-Karpov, Wijk aan Zee 1993 (see diagram 7).

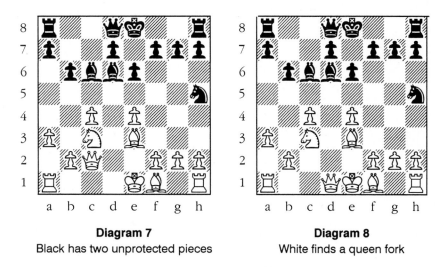

Diagram 7
Black has two unprotected pieces

Diagram 8
White finds a queen fork

Anatoly Karpov, world champion between 1975 and 1985, has

just developed his king's bishop from f8 to d6. This turns out to be one of the worst moves of his career as his American opponent replies with the sneaky **12 Qd1!** (see diagram 8), forking the bishop on d6 and the knight on h5. There is no way to defend against both threats and Black will lose a piece immediately. At grandmaster level the loss of a piece like this is always terminal and Karpov immediately resigned the game.

This example provides a further evidence of how vulnerable undefended pieces can be.

WARNING: Always keep a very close eye on undefended pieces as they are highly vulnerable to tactical thrusts.

This warning acts as a corollary to the previous tip – due to the necessity of escaping from check the king is, effectively, always an undefended piece.

Any piece is capable of carrying out a fork. We have already seen examples of the rook, knight and queen carrying out this tactic. Let us now see how bishops, pawns and even the king can do the same.

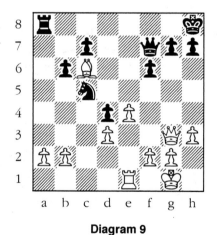

Diagram 9
Can Black capture on a2?

Diagram 10
White forks the queen and rook

In diagram 9 White is a pawn ahead and is threatening the black rook on a8. Black sees a chance to escape from the threat while simultaneously restoring the material balance and plays **1...Rxa2?** However, this walks into a trap. White replies **2 Bd5!** (see diagram 10), forking the queen on f7 and the rook on a2 and will now win material. Note that it is important that the white bishop is protected by the pawn on e4, otherwise Black could simply reply **2...Qxd5**.

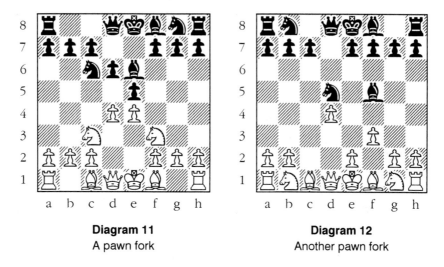

Diagram 11
A pawn fork

Diagram 12
Another pawn fork

Diagrams 11 and 12 see pawn forks in action. In diagram 11 White continues with **1 d5!**, forking the knight on c6 and the bishop on e6, while in diagram 12, **1 e4!** is the killer, again hitting a black knight and bishop.

WARNING: Opportunities for pawn forks often occur early in the game. When you are developing your pieces, keep an eye out for chances for your opponent to attack your pieces with his pawns.

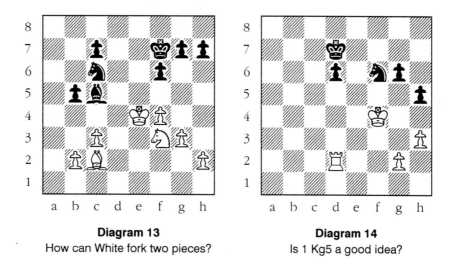

Diagram 13
How can White fork two pieces?

Diagram 14
Is 1 Kg5 a good idea?

The king is perfectly capable of carrying out a fork, although this will usually only occur in the endgame in much simplified positions. Witness the following two examples:

In diagram 13 White can bravely thrust forward with **1 Kd5!** The knight and bishop are both attacked and Black will lose a piece. Finally, diagram 14 provides confirmation that the king is always a tricky piece to handle. White, with the advantage of rook against knight and pawn, is hoping to win. He has the opportunity to continue **1 Kg5?**, forking the knight on f6 and the pawn on g6. Is this a good idea? No! Black will reply with a fork of his own – **1...Ne4+!** Knights are tricky pieces!

The Pin

The second of our tactical tricks is the pin. A pin occurs when you attack a piece which cannot move without exposing another, more valuable, piece behind it to capture. Unlike the fork, a trick which all the pieces can perform, only the long-range pieces – rooks, bishops and queens – are capable of pinning. Let us look at some examples:

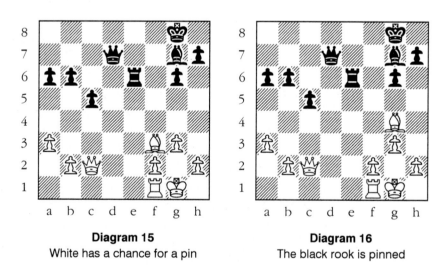

Diagram 15
White has a chance for a pin

Diagram 16
The black rook is pinned

Diagram 15: Here material is level but the black queen and rook have got themselves onto unfortunate squares. With the thrust **1 Bg4!** (see diagram 16), White attacks the black rook which is *pinned* against the black queen. The rook cannot move away without exposing the queen to capture by the white bishop. White will therefore win a rook for a bishop, which should be enough to win the game.

The fork is a device which often wins material immediately, but a pin can take longer to work. Often the pinned piece, although incapable of moving, is protected and cannot be captured immediately.

 TIP: A pinned piece is like an animal caught in a trap. Although it may not be lost at once, its inability to move may prove fatal.

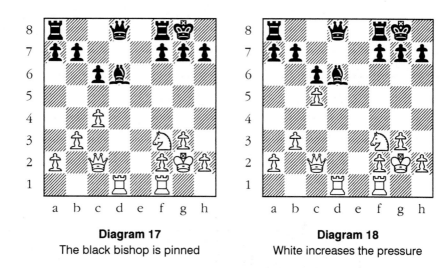

Diagram 17	Diagram 18
The black bishop is pinned	White increases the pressure

In diagram 17 the white rook on d1 pins Black's bishop on d6 against his queen. However, although White cannot gain anything by capturing this piece (1 Rxd6 Qxd6 favours Black), he has a way to exploit the power of the pin. By continuing **1 c5!** (see diagram 18), he brings another attacking unit to bear against the black bishop and leaves his opponent with an insoluble problem. If Black does not move the bishop then White will play 2 cxd6 next move, winning a piece for nothing. However, if he avoids this possibility with, say, **1...Be7** then White has **2 Rxd8**, winning rook for queen, an even greater advantage to that of winning a piece.

Pinning against the King

A very common theme with the pin arises when a piece is pinned against the king. It was noted earlier that a pin is usually made by threatening a lower-ranking piece which cannot move on pain of exposing a higher-ranking piece behind. In a sense, the king is the highest-ranking piece there is and so a pin against the king is particularly nasty.

Again, this is another tactic that often occurs in the opening, particularly along the central files. Witness what happens in diagram 19, which incidentally provides a further indication of why the king is vulnerable in the centre.

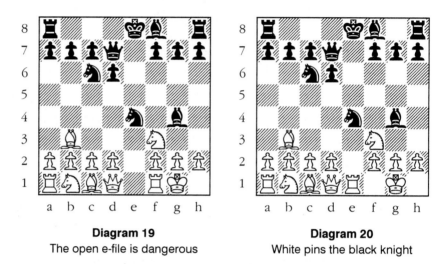

Diagram 19
The open e-file is dangerous

Diagram 20
White pins the black knight

Here the open e-file, combined with the dangerous position of the black king on e8, creates the possiblity for a crushing pin. White continues **1 Re1!** (see diagram 20), attacking the knight on e4 which is pinned against the black king on e8. Black cannot move this knight and, in order to avoid instant material loss, must therefore defend it instead. There are various ways of doing this such as 1...d5, 1...f5 and 1...Bf5. Let us suppose that Black chooses **1...d5**. Now 2 Rxe4+ will get White nowhere – Black will simply capture the rook with the d-pawn with 2...exd4, and White will have lost a rook for a knight – a poor transaction. However, the way to exploit the pin is to bring further pressure to bear on the knight with **2 d3!** (see diagram 21). Now White is threatening to take the knight for a mere pawn and there is nothing that Black can do to prevent it.

Note that Black had a different opportunity on the first move. After **1 Re1!** he could have tried **1...Qe7** which, as well as defending the knight, does actually break the pin (Black can now move the knight without exposing the king to check). However, this would not be any great improvement. White continues along the same lines with **2 d3!** (see diagram 22) and, although Black can now move the knight, doing so will expose his queen to capture by the white rook. So Black will either lose a knight or a queen for a rook – he is caught between the devil and the deep blue sea.

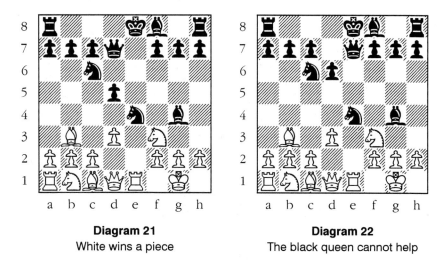

Diagram 21
White wins a piece

Diagram 22
The black queen cannot help

Although it failed in this instance, breaking the pin in such a way is often a good method of dealing with the problem. There are many examples of Black doing just this in the opening. Consider diagram 23, which arises after the common opening sequence **1 e4 e5 2 Nf3 Nf6 3 Nxe5 d6 4 Nf3 Nxe4 5 Qe2**.

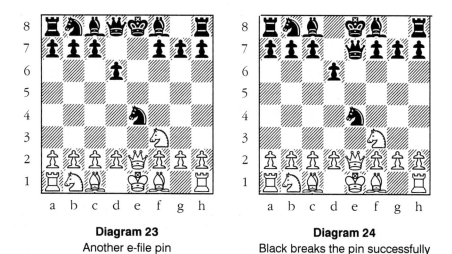

Diagram 23
Another e-file pin

Diagram 24
Black breaks the pin successfully

The black knight is again pinned and attempts to defend it which do not break the pin, such as 5...d5, 5...f5 and 5...Bf5 all fail hopelessly to 6 d3 and White wins a piece. However with **5...Qe7!** (see diagram 24), Black successfully breaks the pin and can meet 6 d3 with 6...Nf6, when White can still capture the black queen, but only at the expense of his own.

The Skewer

The final basic element of tactical play is the skewer. A skewer is really the reverse of a pin. With a pin a lower-ranking piece gets into trouble because it does not want to expose a higher-ranking piece behind. A skewer occurs when a higher-ranking piece is threatened which will expose a lower-ranking piece by moving away. As with the pin, only bishops, rooks and queens can carry out this tactic. Let us look at some examples.

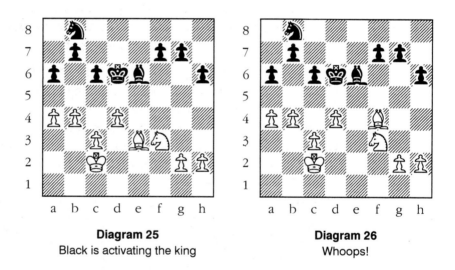

Diagram 25
Black is activating the king

Diagram 26
Whoops!

In diagram 25, Black is trying to activate his king in the endgame. This is usually a good idea, but in this particular instance he has been a little exuberant and when White continues with **1 Bf4+!** (see diagram 26), he finds that his knight has been skewered behind his king.

In diagram 27 Black has a well centralised queen, but he has overlooked the unfortunate placement of this piece *vis-à-vis* the rook on e8. White plays **1 Re1!** (see diagram 28) and Black finds that his rook on e8 has been skewered. Of course he could try **1...Qxe1+**, but after **2 Nxe1** he has suffered the disastrous material loss of a queen for a rook.

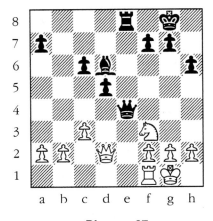

Diagram 27
What is White's best move?

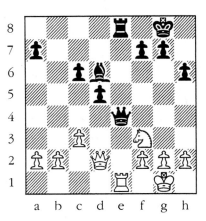

Diagram 28
The queen and rook are skewered

 WARNING: Although it is often a good idea to centralise the queen to increase her power, her great value means that this can make her vulnerable to tactical threats.

Rooks are particularly good at skewering and this tactic often plays a part in endgames. We can see a good example in diagram 29. The important point in this position is that if White can advance his a-pawn to promote on a8, he will win. Black will have to give up his rook for the pawn (now promoted to a queen) and then, with an extra rook, White will win easily.

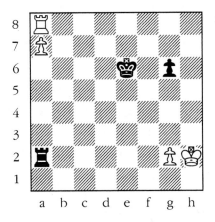

Diagram 29
White is trying to promote the a-pawn

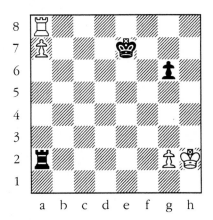

Diagram 30
Black avoids the check

In this position Black seems to be in trouble. White is threatening 1 Re8+ when Black will have no time to capture the a-pawn because he will have to deal with the check. After the black king moves White will be able to promote the pawn and win. Incidentally, note that 1 Re8+ is actually a fork as it creates two threats: the check against the king and the promotion of the pawn.

However it is Black's move, and he finds a good idea to defend against White's threat. He plays **1...Ke7!** (see diagram 30), and if White now tries 2 Re8+? Black can simply capture the rook with 2...Kxe8 and White has got nowhere (Black meets 3 a8Q with 3...Rxa8).

However, White can use the possibility of a skewer to force promotion. He plays the cunning **2 Rh8!** (see diagram 31). He now threatens to promote the pawn and so Black has nothing better than **2...Rxa7**, when White reveals his idea with **3 Rh7+** (see diagram 32), skewering the black rook behind the king.

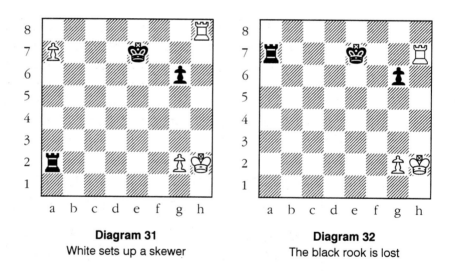

Diagram 31
White sets up a skewer

Diagram 32
The black rook is lost

Countering Tactical Threats

The tactical ideas we have already seen in this chapter – forks, pins and skewers – can be powerful weapons, but you do not necessarily need to despair if you find you have allowed one of them to happen. Chess is a complex game and there are often chances to respond with tactical ideas of your own which can thwart your opponent's intentions. We will now look again at some of the examples used previously in this chapter. By making subtle alterations to the positions, the tactics suddenly become less successful.

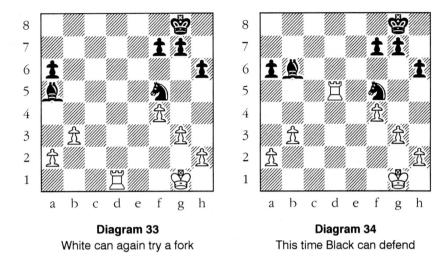

Diagram 33
White can again try a fork

Diagram 34
This time Black can defend

Diagram 33 is very similar to diagram 1, except that the white pawn on f2 has moved forward to f4. If White tries the move that was previously so successful, **1 Rd5**, forking the black bishop and knight, Black can respond **1...Bb6+!** (see diagram 34), and White has no time to capture the knight as he must deal with the check. On his next turn Black can deal with the threat to his knight and he has maintained material equality.

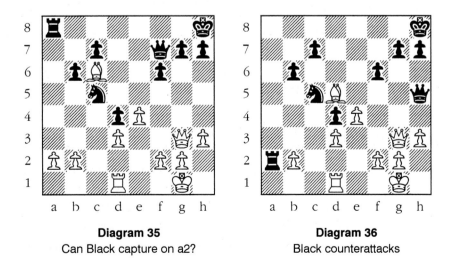

Diagram 35
Can Black capture on a2?

Diagram 36
Black counterattacks

Diagram 35 is a small variation on diagram 9. Black regains his lost pawn with **1...Rxa2**. In our previous example, this worked out badly for Black as White continued with **2 Bd5**, forking the queen and rook. Here the slightly altered position of the white rook creates the chance for a counterattack. Black plays **2...Qh5!** (see diagram 36), hitting the rook on d1. If White now captures the black rook with **3 Bxa2**, then **3...Qxd1+** follows, and Black has regained his lost rook.

TIP: Looking for counter-threats against an opponent's undefended pieces often gives good chances to defeat tactical ploys.

When we looked at the methods of meeting a check, we noted that, as well as moving the king, there were two other possibilities:

a) Capturing the checking piece, and
b) Interposing a piece to block the check.

The same two methods can be used to deal with tactical threats. Diagram 37 is very similar to diagram 15. Instead of a pawn on h7, Black now has a pawn on f7. Nevertheless, this small subtlety makes all the difference. If White again tries his luck with **1 Bg4**, Black can employ a variation on method 'b' above and interpose a pawn with **1...f5!** (see diagram 38). The line of action of the bishop has been cut off and Black will come to no harm as the pawn of f5 is protected by the pawn on g6.

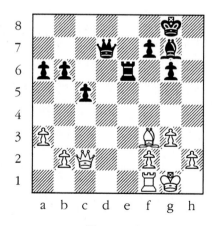

Diagram 37
Will White's pin be successful?

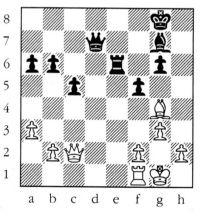

Diagram 38
Black breaks the pin

Our next example (see diagram 39) is a modification of diagram 27. In this position, from the section on the skewer, White's 1 Re1 picked up the black rook on e8. Here the position has been changed slightly by moving the black f-pawn from f7 to f6. Again this makes all the difference. Black can now move his queen in such a way that he can protect the rook on e8. **1 Re1** is met by **1...Qg6!** (see diagram 40), and Black escapes.

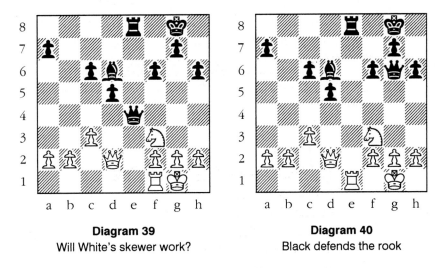

Diagram 39
Will White's skewer work?

Diagram 40
Black defends the rook

Chess can often be a game of cat and mouse, with both players trying to outwit the other in tactical exchanges. Earlier in this chapter we looked at the position arising after the opening sequence **1 e4 c5 2 Nf3 d6 3 c3 Nf6 4 Be2** (see diagram 5).

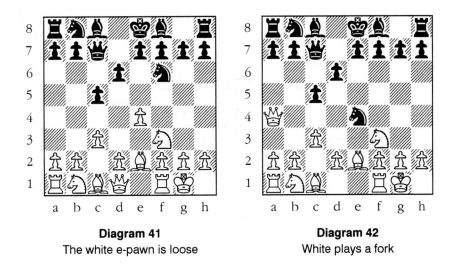

Diagram 41
The white e-pawn is loose

Diagram 42
White plays a fork

Here we noted that White had booby-trapped the e-pawn, as 4...Nxe4 is met by 5 Qa4+ winning a piece with a fork. Let us suppose that Black spots this idea and counters with a tactical idea of his own. He continues with **4...Qc7** and White nonchalantly gets his king to safety with **5 0-0** (see diagram 41).

Black now springs his surprise, capturing the white e-pawn with **5...Nxe4** and when White delivers his fork with **6 Qa4+** (see diagram 42), Black is ready with his counter, **6...Qc6** (see diagram 43).

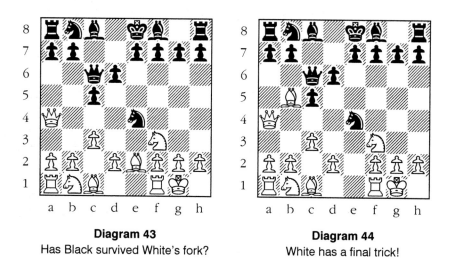

Diagram 43
Has Black survived White's fork?

Diagram 44
White has a final trick!

This looks like a safe win of a pawn for Black. He has blocked the check from the white queen whilst simultaneously protecting his knight on e4. 7 Qxc6+ will get White nowhere (Black can recapture with either knight or pawn) and 7 Qxe4 fails miserably to 7...Qxe4. So has Black turned the tables on his opponent?

No! White has one further trick up his sleeve. Black's 6...Qc6 has placed his queen on a vulnerable diagonal and White exploits this immediately with **7 Bb5!** (see diagram 44). The result is a crushing pin which will result in the win of Black's queen for a mere bishop. Chess is a tricky game!

Try it Yourself

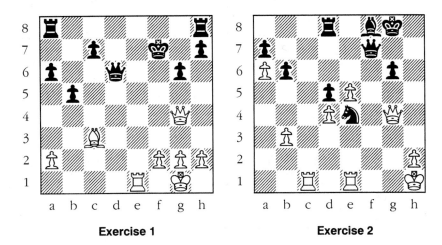

Exercise 1

Exercise 2

Exercise 1: A variation from a game between Garry Kasparov and Viswanathan Anand from their World Championship match in New York 1995. What is White's winning tactic?

Exercise 2: Another possible variation from the above match. How could Anand, Black to play, make a decisive material gain?

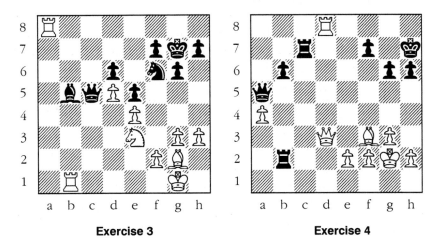

Exercise 3

Exercise 4

Exercise 3: This position features the current British number one, Michael Adams playing Black against Kasparov from a tournament in New York 1995. With a queen against two rooks, Black is not badly off at the moment, but White's next move proved decisive. What was it?

Exercise 4: One of the strongest American players over the past two decades has been Yasser Seirawan. This position is a variation from a win by him against Anatoly Karpov from London 1982. How can White use a fork to set up a mate threat while attacking a black piece?

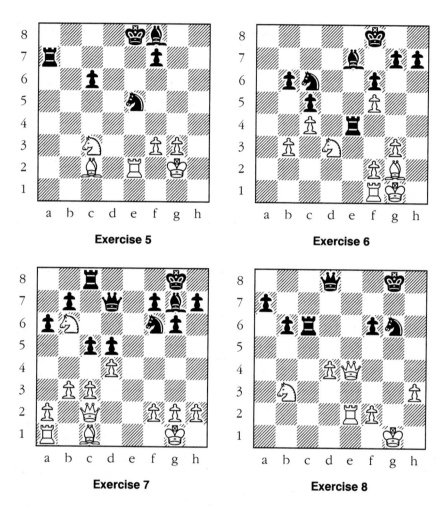

Exercise 5

Exercise 6

Exercise 7

Exercise 8

Exercises 5-8: In the final four exercises, it is Black to play. In each case White has set a tactical problem which Black must deal with. These are a pin (exercise 5), a skewer (exercise 6) and two forks (exercises 7 and 8). Can you find Black's best reply in each case? Be warned – exercise 8 is quite difficult.

Summary

It is often worth pinning a piece, even if you cannot win it immediately. If the pin is strong enough, you may be able to increase the pressure with your next move.

Always keep an eye out for unprotected pieces – both yours and your opponent's. These provide good opportunities for tactics.

When considering a tactical sequence that appears favourable, take a good look at the final position. Your opponent may just have a sting in the tail!

Chapter Seven

Introducing Opening Play

■ Development of the Pieces

■ Influence in the Centre

■ King Safety

Chess is an unusual game in that there is a huge amount of literature devoted to the opening moves and sequences. This literature has developed through many years of both theoretical and practical experimentation. Many opening have exotic names, often taken from the players who developed them or places where they were popularised. Even variations and sub-variations within openings have their own identity.

With so much established theory, the opening in chess is something of a minefield for the newcomer to the game. However, although you cannot hope to learn and understand all the complex ideas in different openings, there are certain basic principles that act as the foundations upon which they are built. An understanding of these principles will provide a good grounding for navigating through the minefield. Three of the most important principles are:

1. Development of the pieces
2. Influence in the centre
3. King safety

Development of the Pieces

Let us look at the starting position (see diagram 1).

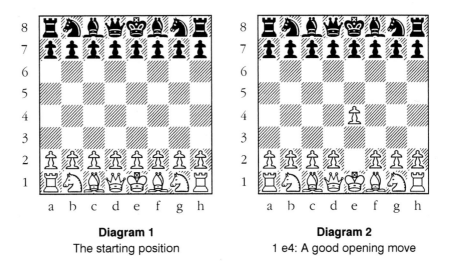

Diagram 1	Diagram 2
The starting position	1 e4: A good opening move

At the moment the pieces have very little mobility. In fact, only the pawns and the knights can actually move. However, this static situation is a temporary one. The pawns will quickly advance and this will free lines for the pieces to emerge. A basic aim in the early part of the game is to mobilise your pieces as quickly as possible. As you mobility increases, you will be better placed to protect yourself against threats from your opponent and to generate such threats yourself.

In Chapter 2, we saw how the pieces had much greater freedom of movement when they were placed in the centre of the board, or at least near to the centre. This principle should guide how we try to develop our pieces. Let us see this in action.

From the starting position White can open with **1 e4** (see diagram 2). This is probably the most popular opening move (1 d4 is also very popular), and with good reason. The pawn is placed in the centre, and lines are opened for the white queen and light-squared bishop to develop. **1...e5** is a very sound reply from Black, for much the same reasons that the white move was good. And now **2 Nf3** (see diagram 3)

Diagram 3
2 Nf3: A good developing move

is another good move and demonstrates two important principles that govern sound developing play:

1. Try to create threats while developing your pieces
2. In general, develop the knights before the bishops.

Let us consider each of these points in turn:

Creating Threats

The reason for the first point should be obvious. If you can develop a piece with a threat, then you will gain time. However, do not get carried away and create threats just for the sake of it. Make sure that your move fits in with what you are trying to achieve and that your threat cannot be easily repulsed by your opponent – if that happens you may simply end up losing time. For example, consider the opening sequence **1 e4 e5** and now a common beginner's move **2 Qh5?** (see diagram 4).

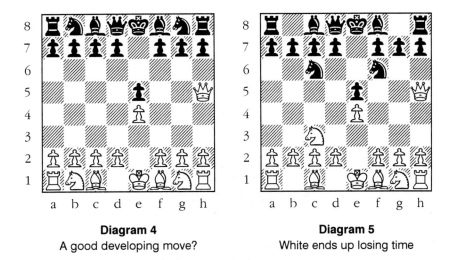

Diagram 4	Diagram 5
A good developing move?	White ends up losing time

Superficially, this looks quite promising. White develops his most powerful piece, substantially increasingly her mobility, and simultaneously creates a threat (3 Qxe5+). So why is this a bad idea? The problem is twofold: firstly it is too early to decide where the queen wants to go; secondly, Black can repulse the threat whilst making natural developing moves. For example, **2...Nc6** defends the e-pawn and after say, **3 Nc3**, Black can gain time himself with **3...Nf6** (see diagram 5). White now finds that he is being kicked around and that his early queen sortie has ended up losing time rather than gaining it.

WARNING: Unless there is a very good reason, do not move the queen early in the game. She will very likely end up being chased around and you will lose time.

Knights before Bishops

The development of the knights first, then bishops is not a strict rule – it is more of a guideline. There are plenty of respectable openings where the placement for a bishop is decided before that of a knight. However, if you have a choice between a knight development and a bishop development it will probably prove better to opt for the knight. To see why this is so let us look at the starting position but remove the e- and d-pawns as they are usually advanced early in the game (see diagrams 6 and 7).

Diagram 6 indicates possible development squares for the f1-bishop. All of these are fine and create good possibilities for this piece. It is also very common to develop this bishop by advancing the g-pawn and placing the bishop on g2 (see diagram 8). This is known as a fianchetto and gives the bishop scope on the long diagonal while also acting as further potential protection for the white king if he decides to castle kingside.

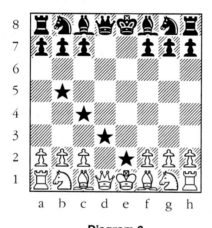

Diagram 6
Possible squares for the bishop

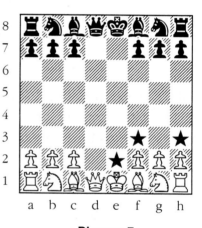

Diagram 7
Possible squares for the knight

However, if we consider the possibilities for the g1-knight (see diagram 7) we can see that it is more than likely that f3 will be the best square. We know that the knight's mobility is dreadfully reduced when it is away from the centre and so h3 is a very unattractive post. The e2-square is better but the influence on the centre is slightly less from here than from f3.

Furthermore, if the f1-bishop is on its starting square, then moving the knight to e2 will hamper the development of this piece. This leads to another useful tip:

TIP: Try to develop your pieces harmoniously. If they are all treading on each other's toes then you may have to waste time relocating them.

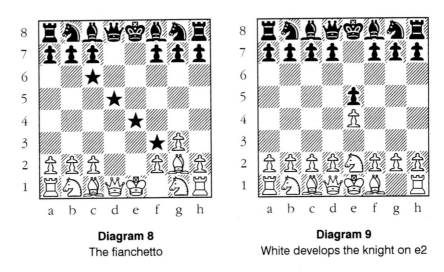

Diagram 8	Diagram 9
The fianchetto	White develops the knight on e2

For example after **1 e4 e5 2 Ne2** (see diagram 9) White will probably have to move this piece again in order to further his development.

Influence in the Centre

This is another key element to chess. The reason we need to have a base in the centre, or at least exert influence there, is that the centre acts as the best jumping-off point to relocate to other areas of the board. If we can establish a strong point in the centre, this will act as a good base for future operations.

Most of the popular openings see both sides establishing some sort of presence in the centre. Let's consider some of these.

The Ruy Lopez

1 e4 e5 2 Nf3 Nc6 3 Bb5 This move identifies the Ruy Lopez and what follows is one of the main lines. **3...a6 4 Ba4 Nf6 5 0-0 Be7 6 Re1 b5 7 Bb3 d6 8 c3 0-0** (see diagram 10). Black has placed a pawn on e5 and constructed his development around it. Both sides have a sound position.

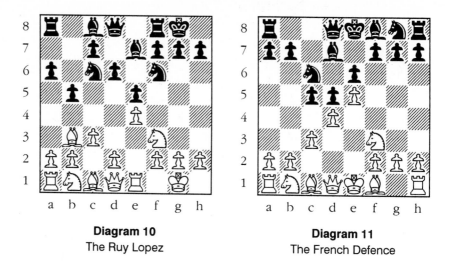

Diagram 10
The Ruy Lopez

Diagram 11
The French Defence

The French Defence

1 e4 e6 2 d4 d5 This is the French Defence. Black establishes a strong point on d5. Note that 1 e4 d5 (although actually a respectable opening) does not achieve this aim as after 2 exd5 Black cannot recapture with a pawn. **3 e5** This is known as the Advance variation. **3...c5 4 c3 Nc6 5 Nf3 Bd7** (see diagram 11). White has more space than Black but Black still has a stronghold in the centre on d5. Chances are balanced.

Diagram 12
The Sicilian Defence

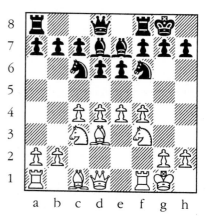

Diagram 13
The opening with no name

The Sicilian Defence

1 e4 c5 This is the Sicilian Defence – the most popular way to meet 1 e4 in contemporary chess. The variation that now arises is known as the Scheveningen. **2 Nf3 d6 3 d4 cxd4 4 Nxd4 Nf6 5 Nc3 e6** (see diagram 12). In contrast to the previous two examples, Black does not have a strongpoint on the fifth rank. However, he has prevented White from establishing a centre with pawns on d4 and e4 and has a good solid structure himself in the form of the pawns on d6 and e6.

The Opening with No Name

1 e4 d6 2 d4 e6 This particular sequence remains without a name – and with good reason! Not only has Black failed to fight for the centre, he has also hemmed in his bishops. **3 c4 Nc6 4 Nc3 Bd7 5 f4** As White is being given free reign in the centre, he sensibly decides to grab as much space as possible. **5...Be7 6 Nf3 Nf6 7 Bd3 0-0 8 0-0** (see diagram 13).

Black's position is not yet a disaster, but it completely lacks dynamism. White has chances, either now or in the near future, to advance with moves such as d4-d5 or e4-e5. Both of these will gain time by driving away the black knights. Black, on the other hand, has nothing much to do. His best idea is to try to arrange either ...d6-d5 or ...e6-e5. However, in this position, both of these will lose a pawn. Black could have decided on one of these advances much earlier. Now he will have to waste time reorganising his position to achieve one of them.

King Safety

Having a secure king is fundamental to a sound poition. The best way to create a safe haven for your king is nearly always to castle. Castling is a great move. It allows you to place the king behind a secure barrier of pawns and to bring a dormant rook into the game. One of the payoffs of developing the f1-bishop and the g1-knight at an early stage is that it clears the back row and enables this move to take place.

The Dangers of delaying Castling

The following two positions were both seen in Chapter 6 (see diagram 14 and 15).

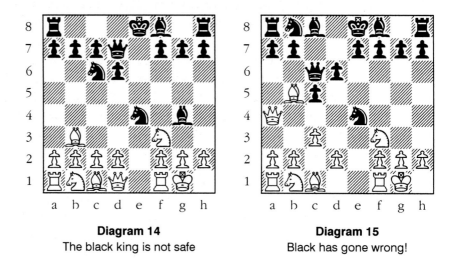

Diagram 14
The black king is not safe

Diagram 15
Black has gone wrong!

Black is about to lose material in both cases and there is a striking feature which is common to both positions: White has secured his king and Black has completely failed to do so. Let us see how each position could have arisen and see where Black could have improved his play:

Example 1: 1 e4 e5 2 Nf3 Nf6 Rather than defending his own e-pawn, Black counterattacks against White's. This is a perfectly good plan and is known as the Petroff Defence. **3 Nxe5 d6 4 Nf3 Nxe4 5 Bc4 Nc6 6 0-0** (see diagram 16)

Diagram 16
Black must get the king safe

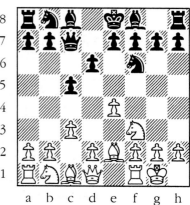

Diagram 17
Black must develop quickly

6...Bg4?! So far the play on both sides has been fine, but this is a step in the wrong direction. Black has formed the plan of castling queenside, but this is a little too slow. A good idea is 6...Be7 when Black is ready to continue with a quick ...0-0 and he will have no problems. **7 Bb3** White could play 7 Re1 but after 7...d5 his own bishop would be attacked and so he brings this piece to a safer square. **7...Qd7?** Black is determined to castle queenside but, as we have seen, this move loses. Black's last chance was 7...Be7, when he will still have time to bring the king to safety on the kingside.

Example 2: 1 e4 c5 2 Nf3 d6 3 c3 This appears to go against the principle of rapid development of the pieces, but White has a clear idea in mind. He wants to continue with d2-d4 on the next move, establishing a strong pawn centre. 3 d4 at once is also possible (and is, in fact, more popular) but after 3...cxd4 White will have to recapture with a piece and thus will not be able to form a broad pawn centre. **3...Nf6 4 Be2** White temporarily shelves the idea of d4, as his e-pawn is threatened. He therefore develops a piece while keeping the tactic 4...Nxe4? 5 Qa4+ in place. **4...Qc7** Although in itself this is far from disastrous, it is a misguided move. As we know it is usually better to develop the minor pieces before the queen and this position is no exception. Black has many decent alternatives here including 4...e6, 4...Nc6 and 4...g6, planning a fianchetto. **5 0-0** (see diagram 17) **5...Nxe4?** As we know this is a blunder which loses a piece, but the seeds of this mistake have already been sown.

Queenside Castling

In certain positions it can be advisable to aim to castle on the queenside. One possible advantage is indicated by the relative positions of the rooks after castling (see diagram 18).

Here the white rook already exerts central pressure along the d-file (it may well be also placed facing the black queen, which could prove useful). Meanwhile, its opposite number is more passively placed on f8. The downside of castling queenside is that it takes a little longer to accomplish – you have to get three pieces out rather than two. Example 1 above demonstrated the potential drawbacks of taking too much time to get the king safe.

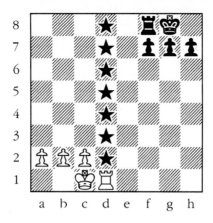

Diagram 18
Castling queenside activates the rook

However, castling queenside can often be a good way to develop as we shall now see. **1 e4 e6 2 d4 d5 3 Nc3 dxe4** Although Black gives up the strongpoint on d5 and has slightly less space than White, he will find it easy to develop his pieces. **4 Nxe4 Nd7 5 Nf3 Ngf6 6 Nxf6+ Nxf6 7 Bd3 Be7 8 Bg5 b6** (see diagram 19) Now a perfectly good way for White to complete his development is a sequence such as 9 0-0 0-0 10 Qd2, planning Rad1. However, White can also be more aggressive and castle queenside, as we shall see. **9 Qe2 Bb7** There is a small but important tactic here. The very natural 9...0-0? fails to 10 Bxf6 Bxf6 11 Qe4 with a fork (threats Qxh7 mate and Qxa8). **10 0-0-0 0-0** (see diagram 20) and White stands well.

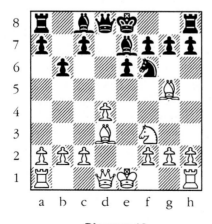

Diagram 19
Where should the white king go?

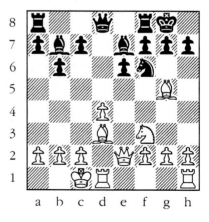

Diagram 20
Castling queenside is a good plan

Summary

Aim to activate your forces quickly. You will need to make some pawn moves to open lines, but do not make too many. Concentrate on developing the pieces.

Establish a strong point in the centre or, if this proves difficult, at least make sure that your pieces are influencing what happens in the centre.

Get you king safe as quickly possible, preferably by castling. If you opponent has neglected to make his king safe look for tactical opportunities to exploit this.

Chapter Eight

Introducing Strategy

- ■ **Why is Strategy Important?**
- ■ **Attacking on Opposite Wings**
- ■ **Play in the Centre**
- ■ **Exploiting Extra Material**

Why is Strategy Important?

An understanding of tactical play is a key element in getting to grips with chess. A feel for tactics enables you to manoeuvre your pieces around without leaving them *en prise* or stumbling into traps. It will also enable you to exploit any similar mistakes that your opponent makes. It is, if you like, an essential survival skill to navigate from one position to another without disaster striking.

Although tactics are a fundamental part of chess, they are very far from being the whole story. Tactical complexity most frequently arises when the two armies are in close contact with each other. However, there are many situations where the two sides are battling at arm's length and there is little opportunity for direct contact. This particularly happens in the early stages of the game, as the two sides are separated by four ranks and hand-to-hand combat does not usually break out until a later stage. It is also perfectly possible for a game to progress for many moves without any great tactical complications arising.

In such situations, when you are in no immediate danger and you cannot create direct threats, calculating tactics is of little use. This is where strategy comes in. You need to have an idea about what you are trying to do in the longer term and to formulate a plan for achieving your aims.

This is a very difficult part of the game to master. Most players with a good feel for chess can pick up tactical ideas quite quickly. However, a feel for strategy is harder to achieve and, to a certain extent, can only develop with experience.

However, efforts in this direction will yield a huge pay-off. A player with limited strategic understanding, but a good grasp of tactics has only one real way to look at a position – they have to analyse everything. They painstakingly wade through a position using the 'I go here, he goes there' method of analysis to find out what works. A good strategic player has less work to do. He will intuitively understand that certain ideas are not strategically viable and so there is no point analysing the nitty-gritty of them. Rather than having to consider ten different tactical ideas in every position he can quickly decide upon a choice between two or three of them. He can then use his thinking time more constructively by quickly selecting a plan and then deciding how to implement it.

So, how do good players decide what to do? Much of this is obviously based on experience, but the motivation for choosing a strategic plan often stems from a consideration of the imbalances in the position. There are two very common imbalances which occur in games. Firstly, one player has the advantage on one wing, but stands worse on the other. In this case we usually see the players attacking on opposite wings. Secondly, it often occurs that one player has the advantage in the centre but has had to make concessions elsewhere. Let us look at examples of each of these in turn.

Attacking on Opposite Wings

Chess is a game where you have to trade advantages. Unless your opponent makes bad mistakes, you will not get something for nothing – instead you will have to barter. For example, many openings allow one player to have the better pawn structure, but the other player has active piece play.

One very common feature of positions is that one side stands well on one wing of the board, while the opposite is the case on the other wing. Such positions often develop into a race. You have to make things happen on 'your' side of the board, while trying to hold up your opponent on the other.

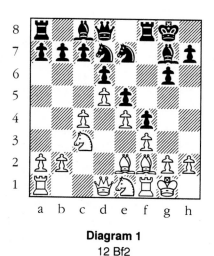

Diagram 1
12 Bf2

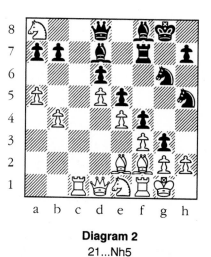

Diagram 2
21...Nh5

Diagram 1 is a standard position from an opening called the King's Indian Defence. White holds the trumps on the queenside while Black has chances to advance on the kingside. The King's Indian Defence has, over the years, been a favourite of Garry Kasparov. Let's see him in action on the black side. The following extract is from the game Piket-Kasparov, played at Tilburg in 1989.

12...g5 13 b4 Nf6 14 c5 Ng6 15 cxd6 cxd6 16 Rc1 Rf7 White is playing to infiltrate along the c-file, whereas Black is looking to prise open the kingside by advancing with ...g5-g4. **17 a4 Bf8 18 a5 Bd7 19 Nb5 g4 20 Nc7 g3!** Although his rook is threatened, Kasparov prefers to continue his kingside initiative. **21 Nxa8 Nh5** (see diagram 2) The fruits of White's queenside play are clear – he has won a rook. However, Kasparov has judged that his initiative on the other wing will be worth this investment and the game proves his judgment to be right. **22 Kh1 gxf2 23 Rxf2 Ng3+! 24 Kg1** If 24 hxg3 fxg3 and the black queen comes to h4. **24...Qxa8 25 Bc4 a6 26 Qd3 Qa7 27 b5 axb5 28 Bxb5 Nh1!** **White resigns** Black's last move forced the win of the rook on f2, after which he will be a piece ahead.

TIP: When the position is unbalanced, look to take the initiative in the area where you are strongest.

In this example the centre was blocked, but advancing on opposite wings can also happen with a more fluid centre.

Diagram 3
15...Ra2

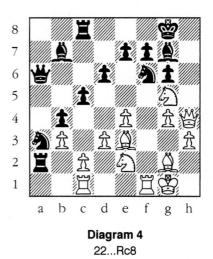

Diagram 4
22...Rc8

Diagram 3 is another typical position for attacking on opposite wings. The game Spassky-Geller, played in the World Championship Quarter-Finals in 1968, continued: **16 g4 Qa8 17 Qe1 Qa6 18 Qf2 Na7** White is ferrying pieces over to the kingside in the expectation of effecting a breakthrough, while Black is doing the same on the opposite wing. **19 f5 Nb5 20 fxg6 hxg6 21 Ng5 Na3 22 Qh4 Rc8** (see diagram 4) Black has broken through and White's queenside is about to collapse. However, Black's play has been a little slow and White now has a decisive superiority of force on the kingside. **23 Rxf6! exf6 24 Qh7+ Kf8 25 Nxf7! Rxc2** If 25...Kxf7 26 Bh6 Rg8 27 Nf4 and White's threats are too strong. **26 Bh6 Rxc1+ 27 Nxc1 Kxf7 28 Qxg7+ Ke8 29 g5!** After this Black's king is easy prey. **29...f5 30 Qxg6+ Kd7 31 Qf7+ Kc6 32 exf5+ Black resigns**

Play in the Centre

A position can also be unbalanced when one player holds the advantage in the centre but has made concessions elsewhere.

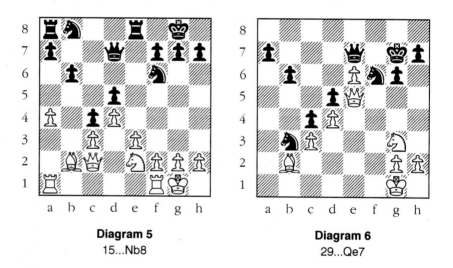

Diagram 5
15...Nb8

Diagram 6
29...Qe7

Diagram 5 arose in a game played in Amsterdam in 1938 between two great World Champions. White was Mikhail Botvinnik and Black was José Raoul Capablanca. The position is a typical one from an opening called the Nimzo-Indian Defence.

Looking at the pawn structure we can see that White has a superiority in the centre, but that Black has the advantage on the queenside. Furthermore, White's a-pawn is rather weak and exposed. This gives us a clue to the following play. White will advance in the centre and Black will try to invade on the queenside. **16 Rae1 Nc6 17 Ng3 Na5 18 f3** White wants to advance with e3-e4 but must ensure that in the event of ...d5xe4 he can recapture with a pawn and maintain a solid pawn front. **18...Nb3 19 e4 Qxa4 20 e5** So Black has won a pawn on the queenside, but White has carried out his central advance. **20...Nd7 21 Qf2 g6 22 f4 f5 23 exf6 Nxf6 24 f5 Rxe1 25 Rxe1 Re8 26 Re6 Rxe6 27 fxe6 Kg7 28 Qf4 Qe8 29 Qe5 Qe7** (see diagram 6) White's central initiative has yielded a powerful pawn on e6 but it appears that Black has successfully blocked the further advance of this pawn. However, White now destroys this blockade with a brilliant combination. **30 Ba3! Qxa3 31 Nh5+! gxh5 32 Qg5+ Kf8 33 Qxf6+ Kg8 34 e7 Qc1+** White is threatening Qf8 mate and e8Q mate. Black cannot counter both threats and so his only chance is a desperate attempt to gain perpetual check. **35 Kf2 Qc2+ 36 Kg3 Qd3+ 37 Kh4 Qe4+ 38 Kxh5 Qe2+ 39 Kh4 Qe4+ 40 g4 Qe1+ 41 Kh5 Black resigns** White has escaped the perpetual check and Black has no defence.

A superiority in the centre can also act as a springboard for a kingside attack, as we see in the following example.

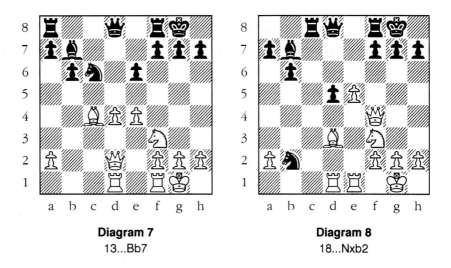

Diagram 7	Diagram 8
13...Bb7	18...Nxb2

Diagram 7 occurred in a game between Lev Polugaevsky (White) and Mikhail Tal (Black) played in the USSR

Championship in 1969. At first sight it looks as if White is well on top. He has a beautiful centre and his pieces are well developed. It is true that White does have a good position, but Black is not badly placed himself. He has managed to develop his pieces comfortably and he has a 2-1 pawn majority on the queen's wing which he can hope to utilise at a later stage. **14 Rfe1 Na5 15 Bd3 Rc8 16 d5** White sacrifices a pawn to open up lines towards the black king. White has noticed that the black kingside is short of defenders and wants to ferry his pieces over there as quickly as possible. **16...exd5 17 e5 Nc4 18 Qf4 Nb2** (see diagram 8) **19 Bxh7+!** This is a typical sacrifice to prise the black king out from behind his pawn cover. **19...Kxh7 20 Ng5+ Kg6** Retreating is no better as after 20...Kg8 21 Qh4 Re8 22 Qh7+ Kf8 23 e6, White has an overwhelming attack. **21 h4 Rc4 22 h5+ Kh6 23 Nxf7+ Kh7 24 Qf5+ Kg8 25 e6 Qf6 26 Qxf6 gxf6 27 Rd2 Rc6 28 Rxb2 Re8 29 Nh6+ Kh7 30 Nf5 Rexe6 31 Rxe6 Rxe6** Black has done well to escape into an ending. However, White's active pieces and Black's weak pawns ensure that he will not last very long. **32 Rc2 Rc6 33 Re2 Bc8 34 Re7+ Kh8 35 Nh4 f5 36 Ng6+ Kg8 37 Rxa7 Black resigns**

TIP: If you have a good central position look to see if this can be used as the basis for a direct attack against the king.

The best way to further your strategic understanding of positions is to play through games (preferably with annotations) by the top players and try to get a feel for what both sides are trying to achieve. Sometimes such games may be highly complex and the tactical play may appear to be impenetrable. However, you should not be too concerned about this. A greater understanding of tactics and a better feel for the interaction of the pieces will come as your strength improves. The important thing is to try to gain a sense of what you ought to be trying to do in different positions. Even if you cannot handle the tactical play like the great masters, at least you can console yourself with the fact that your objectives are the same!

As we have already discussed, a good grasp of strategy will also save you the bother of looking at ideas which just won't work. For example, in diagram 3, a player unfamiliar with this kind of position might think to themselves: 'Well, my rook isn't doing much on c1 – maybe I should try to activate it by advancing c2-c4.' Or perhaps their thought processes might lead them to feel that they had to try to play d3-d4 at some points. A player who understands this structure better will know that these ideas are highly unlikely to be successful. They will know that play on the kingside is indicated and can spend their time more constructively in considering the different methods by which such a plan might be implemented.

Exploiting Extra Material

One problem that often baffles newcomers to the game is how to win the game when you have extra material. Let us assume that the game has gone well and you have won something – how do you go about converting your advantage?

The basic principle here is to exchange pieces. The reason for this is simple mathematics. If you have five units and your opponent four your relative advantage in firepower is only 25%. However, if you can exchange three units, leaving you with two against one, suddenly your advantage increases to 100%!

Remember that you can win a game easily with just one extra pawn. A pawn more does not sound like much, but when the position becomes simplified, that extra pawn can become a queen. Diagram 9 demonstrates this.

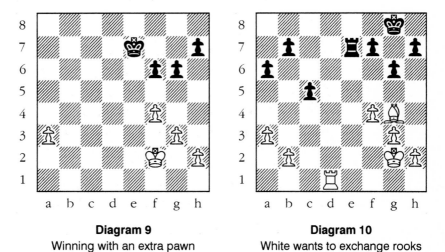

Diagram 9	**Diagram 10**
Winning with an extra pawn	White wants to exchange rooks

White has 'only' one pawn more, but will win the game easily. In fact, an experienced player on the black side would not even bother to play on here and would resign. White's plan is very simple: he will advance his a-pawn; to stop this pawn Black will have to move his king over to the queenside; White's king will then be able to invade the kingside and capture Black's pawns, freeing the way for his own kingside pawns to promote.

However, what if your opponent refuses to co-operate and will not exchange pieces? Well, then make sure that yours are placed on good posts. If your opponent doesn't want to make exchanges, his pieces will have to scurry off to the sidelines and your forces will become even more powerful.

In diagram 10 White has an extra piece and should win easily. The best plan is with **1 Rd7**, offering to swop rooks. If Black wants to decline, he will have to move his rook away from the seventh rank and the black pawn on b7 will fall at once.

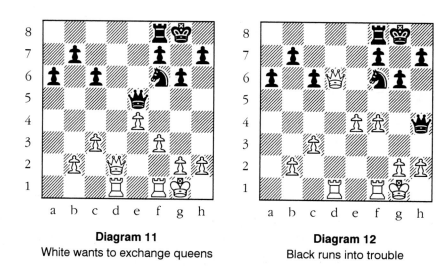

Diagram 11
White wants to exchange queens

Diagram 12
Black runs into trouble

In diagram 11, White's task is more difficult. Here the advantage is rook for knight, quite enough to win, but with other pieces on the board the process is more complex. White starts with **1 Qd6**. This is a good, sensible move, centralising the queen. Black would like to keep the queens on to increase the chances of stirring up trouble but in this case it is not possible. Black's knight is also loose and the only move of the queen that keeps it protected is **1...Qg5**. However, White can now play **2 f4** when **2...Qh4** is forced (see diagram 12). Note that Black's attempts to keep the queens on have led to his queen being forced away from the centre. He now pays a price for this as White continues **3 g3** and the black knight is lost.

Summary

To a certain extent an understanding of strategy can only come with experience. Playing through games by the top players will help you acquire this experience.

Try to take the initiative in the area of the board where you are strongest.

A strong position in the centre often creates the opportunity for a direct attack against the king.

When you are material ahead, aim for exchanges.

Chapter Nine

Inside the Chess World

- **The World Chess Championship**
- **Ratings and Titles**
- **Chess on the Internet**
- **Chess and Computers**

Having read and played through the earlier material in this book you now have a good grounding for playing the game competitively and also for having an understanding of what strong players are looking out for and trying to achieve in their games. However, chess is not played in a vacuum – it is a fascinating game with a rich history and culture. The intention behind this final chapter is to give a feel for the history of the game and the modern developments.

The World Chess Championship

The World Championship in chess was initiated in 1886, since which time, apart from a brief gap at the end of the Second World War, there has always been a player recognised as world champion. In the years up until the end of 1946, this player was expected to play matches to defend the title against the leading challengers of the day. However, there was no formal structure to enable players to qualify for matches against the incumbent champion and this enabled some of the champions to avoid their more dangerous contemporaries or postpone the matches. After Alexander Alekhine's death (as world champion) in 1946, the World Chess Federation (FIDE) stepped in and organised a five-player tournament (won by Mikhail Botvinnik) to determine the new champion. They also established a structure of tournaments and matches to decide a challenger to the champion. In general, this resulted in a match for the World Championship every three years.

In the years up until the early seventies, the World Championship was utterly dominated by Soviet players and thus failed to capture the imagination of the Western public. However, all this changed dramatically in 1972 when chess first received major media exposure thanks to the exploits of the mercurial American genius Bobby Fischer. In 1972 Fischer defeated the Russian Boris Spassky in a match in Reykjavik and thus became the first non-Soviet to hold the world title since the Second World War. In 1975, Fischer defaulted his title when he was unable to agree terms to play a match against his challenger, the Russian Anatoly Karpov. Karpov had gained the right to challenge Fischer by defeating fellow Russian Viktor Korchnoi, who was soon to defect to the West. In 1978 and 1981 Karpov and Korchnoi played two further matches for the

World Championship, both of which were won by Karpov.

Karpov's next challenger was Garry Kasparov. Historically, matches for the World Championship had been played as the best of 24 games. However, the first match between Karpov and Kasparov was played as an open-ended contest with the condition that the first player to achieve six wins would become champion. This match developed into a war of attrition and staggered on for an extraordinary six months before it was controversially halted, 'without result', by the then FIDE (World Chess Federation) President, Florencio Campomanes. The two players played a re-match in 1985, which was won by Kasparov. Kasparov went on to win further matches between the two players in 1986, 1987 and 1990.

All three of these rivalries succeeded in capturing the public imagination, most probably because their battles transcended the chessboard and led them to be seen as a metaphor for a wider context. The Fischer–Spassky clash was played at the height of the Cold War with both champions being perceived as the finest products of their respective ideologies. The Karpov–Korchnoi clashes (played between 1974 and 1981) had resonance as Karpov was a Russian hero of the pre-glasnost era while Korchnoi represented the disaffected dissident. Finally, Garry Kasparov, who usurped Karpov's title in 1985, was a symbol of the new Russia which was emerging under Gorbachov, whereas Karpov was seen to represent the old regime of die-hard Communists such as Brezhnev.

In 1993, Karpov's perennial role in World Championship matches was ended when he lost in the qualifiers to Nigel Short of England who went on to acquire the right to challenge Garry Kasparov for the world title. However, the two players became involved in a dispute with FIDE, the organising body, and therefore broke away to form their own rival organisation, the Professional Chess Association (PCA). Their 1993 match, which resulted in a comfortable win for Kasparov, was played under the auspices of this new organisation. FIDE, meanwhile, organised its own match, played between the runners-up in the qualifying cycle. This match was contested by Karpov and Jan Timman of the Netherlands and was won easily by Karpov.

Kasparov subsequently defended his PCA title against

Viswanathan Anand of India in New York in 1995. However, the PCA was soon disbanded and replaced with a new Kasparov organisation, the World Chess Council which has, at the time of writing (late 1999), proved unable to organise a World Championship match. Although he has not defended his title for some time, in the first half of 1999 Kasparov achieved three decisive first places in tournaments that featured all the best players in the world. This, combined with the fact that he is rated much higher than anybody else demonstrates that he is unquestionably the strongest player in the world. However, he is not the world champion of the official governing body.

The roll of honour for the World Chess Championship since 1886 reads as follows:

Dates	Champion	Nationality
1886-1894	Wilhelm Steinitz	Austria
1894-1921	Emanuel Lasker	Germany
1921-1927	José Raoul Capablanca	Cuba
1927-1935	Alexander Alekhine	USSR and France
1935-1937	Max Euwe	Netherlands
1937-1946	Alexander Alekhine	USSR and France
1948-1957	Mikhail Botvinnik	USSR
1957-1958	Vassily Smyslov	USSR
1958-1960	Mikhail Botvinnik	USSR
1960-1961	Mikhail Tal	USSR
1961-1963	Mikhail Botvinnik	USSR
1963-1969	Tigran Petrosian	USSR
1969-1972	Boris Spassky	USSR
1972-1975	Bobby Fischer	USA
1975-1985	Anatoly Karpov	USSR
1985-	Garry Kasparov	USSR/Russia

Although Garry Kasparov is universally recognised as the strongest player in the world, Anatoly Karpov was the FIDE World Champion from 1993-1999, when he was succeeded by Alexander Khalifman. Khalifman won the title by virtue of winning a large knockout tournament. This format for deciding the World Champion is a recent innovation by FIDE.

Ratings and Titles

Sports and games enthusiasts like to compare the favourite players and thus nowadays virtually all sports have ranking systems for the top players. These are often, however, based on not altogether satisfactory premises. Typical examples of the clumsy devices that are used to rank players are: prize money won; ranking points awarded from events more or less arbitrarily; while even peculiar mathematical formulae, the workings of which are too obscure for easy comprehension, are often employed.

Chess Ratings

Chess, on the other hand, has an excellent system for ranking players. It was developed by the Hungarian mathematician Dr. Arpad Elo and is, in essence, quite simple. It ranks all players in the international arena by taking account of all games played during a fixed period of time. Traditionally, the resulting 'Elo list' used to be updated every six months but, with the advent of computer technology, this has become much more frequent.

The Elo system works by allotting each player a number which is typically between 2200 (the standard for an international player) and 2800 (typical world champion rating). When a player competes in a tournament the average Elo rating of their opposition is calculated. A simple mathematical formula is then applied to determine what their 'par' score against such opposition should be. For example, a player ranked 2400, playing against opposition ranked 2600, would only be expected to score 25%. If the player out-performs their par score, they will gain points and, conversely, they will lose points for a sub-standard result.

Very properly, the Elo system reflects the fact that the road to chess mastery is a long one. The system is what might loosely be termed 'conservative' – it is very unusual to gain more than about 50 points in a year (however, as many players will testify, losing a large number of points is often less difficult). If a player rated a mere 2400 performs at the level of the world champion in one tournament (unlikely, but not unheard of), they will still be unlikely to gain more than about 50 points. Therefore, when a player attains a high rating it is almost certainly the result of several years of progress rather than a couple of spectacular results.

The Elo Rating System

The following table provides an indication of the approximate strength of players at different ratings.

Rating	Strength
2800	World Champion
2700	World Championship Candidate
2600	Strong Grandmaster
2500	Typical Grandmaster
2400	International Master
2300	FIDE (World Chess Federation) Master
2200	International player
2100	Strong County player
2000	Strong Club player
1800	Good Club player
1600	Moderate Club player
1400	Strong Social player
1200	Moderate Social player
1000	Beginner

Titles

The above table indicates the approximate strength of a player who has achieved a particular rating. In addition to achieving high ratings, players also strive to attain international titles – the chess equivalent of Doctorates and PhDs. Originally, grandmaster status was conferred more or less arbitrarily upon players whose play seemed to merit such recogonition. Now, however, there are three recognised titles and the whole issue has been placed on a strict mathematical basis, which is closely allied to the Elo rating system. The three titles (from the bottom to top) are: FIDE Master, International Master (IM) and Grandmaster (GM). The FIDE Master title does not require any specific tournament performances and is awarded to anyone who achieves a rating of 2300.

The requirement for the IM title is more complex but essentially boils down to the following. A tournament performance of 2450+ yields what is known as an 'IM norm'. It is necessary to obtain three of these (although sometimes two is permissible if the tournaments are of sufficient length) and, additionally, to attain a published rating of 2400+. (Remember that a single tournament performance, no matter how good, will usually only make a slight alteration to a published rating.) The requirements for the GM title are similar, although the bar is obviously raised. The tournament performances must be of 2600+ standard and the published rating must be 2500+.

Once a title has been obtained it is never relinquished. If you obtain the grandmaster title you will always be a grandmaster, regardless of your recent results or current rating. There are currently more than 400 Grandmasters in the world and more than 1,000 International Masters.

Chess on the Internet

The extraordinary development and growth of the Internet over the past few years has created new opportunities in all activities, and chess is no exception. This is not surprising as chess is almost perfectly suited to the kind of interaction that the Internet enables. Initially this new technology was used by the chess community as a mechanism for exchanging information. Tournament results were posted on websites and games were analysed and discussed in newsgroups.

However, as the technology improved, new horizons opened up and it is now possible to follow games played in tournaments in real time. Even speed games, where moves are made every few seconds, are easy enough to link into directly. Playing games over an internet connection is also very popular and there are now several sites that offer this facility, some of which encourage the participation of several of the world's leading grandmasters.

It is now quite common for exhibition matches to be played over the Internet. In early 1999, Garry Kasparov and Vladimir Kramnik, currently ranked first and third in the world respectively, played such a match. It was contested as the best of 24 games and each player had just five minutes for the entire game. The games could be accessed in real time and, not surprisingly, these drew a huge audience. When Kasparov famously lost the final game of his match against IBM's Deep Blue computer in May 1997, the IBM site recorded 20 million hits during play. In contrast, the main website for the Atlanta Olympics of 1996 received 'only' 10 million hits for the entire two-week duration of the event.

The Internet is a very promising development for gaining a wider audience for chess. Historically, television coverage of chess has, understandably, been patchy as the excitement of chess is difficult to convey using this means. However, for enthusiasts, the Internet is probably an even better medium for following chess than television. The moves can be followed on a graphical board which is updated automatically. It is also possible to follow expert commentary or even discuss the current games in chat rooms.

Many sports have made an attempt to transfer the excitement to the Internet. For example, it is possible to follow live the intricate details of all plays in American Football matches. This is a tremendous achievement but I can imagine that, for a die-hard fan, there is nothing quite like actually being at the match. In chess this is not necessarily the case. It may seem a little anti-social, but following chess matches at home on a computer can be just as exciting as actually being there.

Chess and Computers

Computers have now been with us for about 50 years but, for much of that time, their attempts at chess were somewhat laughable. They were just about okay for complete beginners but they were not expected to provide a worthwhile opponent for even a weak club player. Now, however, all this has changed. Even the great Garry Kasparov has admitted that, in certain chess positions where the emphasis is on tactics, the silicon brain is superior to the human. It is no longer surprising to see computers holding their own against even the world's very best.

The explosion in the strength of computers has had profound implications for opening preparation – a vital element in international chess. Finding a powerful new move in a sharp variation can sometimes lead to an effortless win. Players will spend much of their preparation time looking for such opportunities and even world-class grandmasters are no longer embarrassed to admit that many of their best ideas have been found in consultation with their PCs.

However, chessplaying programs can also be effectively used by players of all standards. When set to their highest level, almost all commercial programs are now far too strong for about 99.999% of the chessplaying public. However, all programs have a facility to turn off the heat by easing down their playing strength. Most also have the ability to perform other useful tasks, such as suggesting moves, demonstrating what their threats are and indicating which squares are threatened by which pieces. All of these are very helpful to players trying to improve their feel for the game.

As many people will testify, doing anything that involves computers can be quite addictive and playing chess against them is no exception. However, it is not a terribly good way to improve your game at whatever level you are playing. Computers play in a completely different style to human opponents. A typical pattern for a match between a human and a computer is as follows:

1. A new game starts. The program demonstrates strategic incompetence and the human gains a big advantage.

2. The human loses some control over the position and a flurry of tactics occur.

3. The machine finds an amazing resource, turns the game around and wins.

4. The human gets very unhappy and returns to '1'.

This can continue for a long time.

However, there are ways to play against a computer constructively. For example, you can set up positions with simple winning endgames and try to force the win. Not many chessplayers will be prepared to sit around all day defending inferior endgames but a computer is more than happy to do so. This makes it an invaluable sparring partner.

Chapter Ten

Solutions to Exercises

Chapter Two: Solutions

Exercise 1

a) The white rook can move to b4, d4, e4, c3 and c2. It can also capture the black bishops on a4 and c5.

b) The black knight can move to d7 and h7. It can also capture the white bishop on e6.

Exercise 2

a) The white queen can move to a5, b7, c8, b5, c4, d3 and e2. It can also capture the black knight on f1.

b) The black bishop can move to g2, g4, f5 and e6. It can also capture the white pawn on d7.

Exercise 3

The white king has five available moves, including captures. It can move to b2, b4, c4 and d3 as well as being able to capture the knight on d4. The black king has four possibilities: moving to g7, g5 and h5, or capturing the white pawn on g6. Therefore the white king has more moves available.

Exercise 4

a) The white pawn on a2 can move to a3 or a4 and can also capture the black bishop on b3. The white pawn on f4 has only one move available – it can advance one square to f5.

b) The black pawn on c6 has no forward moves available but it can capture the white knight on d5. The black pawn on h5 is in a similar situation. It cannot advance but it can make a capture – in this case the white rook on g4.

Exercise 5

Each of the white pawns has two possible moves available – advancing one square or two. As there are eight pawns this makes a total of 16 moves. All the other pieces are boxed in and have no moves available with the exception of the knights, each of which has two possible moves. The knight on b1 can go to a3 or c3 and the knight on g1 can go to h3 or f3. Thus White can choose from 16 pawn moves and four knight moves for a total of 20.

Exercise 6

a) There is only one way of doing this and it effectively demonstrates the long range ability of the queen: g2-a8-a1.

b) Again, there is only one way to achieve this: h8-h5-a5-a1.

Exercise 7

The white king can move only to g1, all other squares being covered by either the black queen or bishop (e1 is occupied by the white knight). The black king also has only one move available – the capture of the white rook on d7. Therefore both kings have only one possible move.

Exercise 8

It takes the white knight four moves to capture either pawn, e.g. a1-b3-d4-e2xc3 or a1-b3-d4-e6xg7.

Chapter Three: Solutions

Exercise 1

a) White can castle queenside, but not kingside. The black bishop covers the f1-square and prevents the latter move.

b) Conversely, Black can castle kingside, but not queenside. The white pawn on c7 threatens the d8-square and thus prevents Black from playing ...0-0-0.

Exercise 2

White can promote the e-pawn either by advancing to e8 or by capturing the black bishop on d8. If the pawn advances to e8 then promoting to a queen or bishop will both give check. If White captures on d8 and is determined to give check, then only promotion to a knight will do the trick.

Exercise 3

The c2-pawn is blocked by the bishop on c1 and cannot promote at all. The d2-pawn can promote by capturing the white bishop on c1. However, it cannot advance to d1, as this would expose the black king to check from the white bishop on c1. The f2-pawn cannot promote on f1 (the white rook prevents this), nor can it capture the white knight on g1 as this would result in a check to the black king from the white rook.

Exercise 4

White can make the *en passant* capture by playing **1 cxd6**. Although it conforms to the rules of *en passant*, 1 exd6 is not possible as this leaves the white king in check.

Chapter Four: Solutions

Exercise 1

Upper diagram: White can give checkmate in one move only by playing **1 Qe7**.

Lower diagram: White's only checkmating move is **1 Qf1**. Note that 1 Qd2+ would not be checkmate as Black could reply 1...exd2.

Exercise 2

Upper diagram: White's checkmating move is **1 Ng6**.

Lower diagram: White can mate in one move with **1 Bb3**.

Exercise 3

Upper left – stalemate; upper right – not stalemate, Black can play **1...Kg8**; lower left – not stalemate, Black can play **1...Ka2**; lower right – not stalemate, Black has no king moves, but can play **1...gxf3**.

Exercise 4

Upper diagram: White can force perpetual check with **1 Qe8+ Kh7 2 Qh5+ Kg8 3 Qe8+ Kh7 4 Qh5+** etc.

Lower diagram: Here White has a clever way to force a perpetual check which also involves a mating idea. White plays **1 Nh2+ Ke1 2 Nf3+ Kf1 3 Nh2+ Kg1**. Black has had no success with moving to e1 and so tries the other direction. However, after **4 Nf3+** if Black tries to escape by running into the corner with 4...Kh1 then 5 Rh2 is checkmate! Therefore Black must reconcile himself to **4...Kf1 5 Nh2+** and perpetual check.

Chapter Five: Solutions

Exercise 1

The following captures are possible: 1 Rxa8, 1 Bxe6 and 1

Bxc7. 1 Rxa8 is met by 1...Nxa8 and 1 Bxe6 is met by 1...Nxe6 when, in both cases, the game remains equal. However, **1 Bxc7!** wins White a piece for nothing.

Exercise 2

White has a number of captures here: 1 Nxc7, 1 Qxc8, 1 Qxg6, 1 Qxb4 and 1 Bxa8. 1 Nxc7 is no good after 1...Qxc7. Of the three queen captures only 1 Qxc8 Raxc8 keeps the game equal. Both black minor pieces are protected by pawns and the capture of either of these would cost White the queen. The best move is **1 Bxa8!** Black can recapture with 1...Qxa8, but the rook is more valuable than the bishop. Note that Black can meet 1 Bxa8 with 1...Qxg4, but White recaptures with 2 hxg4 and maintains material superiority.

Exercise 3

The safe squares for the rook are d5, e4 and g4.

Exercise 4

White has only one square where the rook can safely move – h5. However, White has another method of meeting the queen threat. The rook can be defended and there are two ways to accomplish this: **1 Bd3** and **1 g4**.

Exercise 5

Black can move the bishop, although the only possible square is d7. Black cannot defend the bishop directly, but the move **1...Nbd7** opens up the back rank, allowing the rook on a8 to protect the bishop. Finally, Black can safely block the line of attack with **1...Ne6**.

Exercise 6

The black queen has no safe squares to move to, so Black must block the line of attack. There are three ways to do this: 1...Be6, 1...Ne6 and 1...Re6. The first two are bad as they leave the piece on e6 pinned. White will continue with 2 f5 and the pinned piece will be lost. The best defence is **1...Re6!** This piece is not pinned (2 f5 can be met by 2...Rxe1+) and White has no good continuation.

Exercise 7

The black knight has no squares to move to, it cannot be defended and the line of attack cannot be blocked. However, Black can use a check to relocate the rook to a more favourable square with **1...Rd1+!** when **2 Kh2** is White's only move. Now the black rook is on a better square and can move again with **2...Ra1**, when the knight is protected.

Exercise 8

In this example blocking the line of attack immediately does not work (1 Nc3 is met by 1...Bxc3 and 1 Bd4 is met by 1...Bxd4). However, by flicking in a check with **1 Rd1+!** White brings added protection to the d4-square. After, for example, **1...Kc8 2 Bd4**, White has successfully blocked the attack.

Chapter Six: Solutions

Exercise 1

White, who is a rook for bishop down on material, could regain this by playing 1 Bxh8. However, he has something much better. White plays **1 Qf3+!**, forking the black king and rook on a8. Note that although this rook is currently protected by its colleague on h8, Black will have to break this contact by playing his king to the back rank to escape from the check with **1...Kg8**. White then plays **2 Qxa8+** and will win quickly.

Exercise 2

The material situation is balanced, but Black changes all that with **1...Nf2+!**, forking the white king and queen.

Exercise 3

White is slightly ahead on material, having a pair of rooks against the black queen. However, Kasparov spotted the chance for a killing pin with **1 Ra5!** The black bishop on b5 is pinned against the queen and White will win a whole piece, which will leave him with a decisive material advantage.

Exercise 4

The key factors in this position are the exposed black king and the unprotected rook on b2. White can set up a fork with **1**

Qd4! This threatens both 2 Rh8 mate (or 2 Qh8 mate) and 2 Qxb2. A try for Black in reply is **1...Qc3**. This blocks the attack against the rook and prevents 2 Qh8 (2 Qh8+ Qxh8). However it does nothing to prevent **2 Rh8** which is still checkmate.

Exercise 5

Black must defend the knight on e5 which is attacked by the white rook and pinned against the black king. There are various ways of doing this, but only one is successful. 1...Ra5, 1...f6, 1...Bd6 and 1...Bg7 defend the knight in the short term but fail to break the pin. White steps up the pressure with 2 f4 and the knight will be lost.

The only way to protect the knight and break the pin is **1...Re7!** when **2 f4** can be met by a knight move, e.g. **2...Nd7**.

Exercise 6

White has skewered the black knight behind the black rook. One way to escape a skewer is to move the immediately threatened piece and use it to defend the piece behind. Here Black has a way to do this: 1...Re6. However, this move is disastrous on account of 2 fxe6 winning a rook for nothing.

The way for Black to solve his problems is by launching a counterattack: **1...Rd4!** This threatens the white knight and allows Black to meet **2 Bxc6** with **2...Rxd3**, maintaining material equality. If White moves the knight instead, Black can simply move his own knight and has again suffered no harm.

Exercise 7

The black queen and knight are forked. One possibility for counterplay is 1...Qf5, threatening the white queen on c2. Then 2 Nxc8 fails to 2...Qxc2. However, after 1....Qf5 White simply captures the black queen with 2 Qxf5 and if 2...gxf5 3 Nxc8 and White has won a rook.

Looking around the position for other possibilities, we notice that White has a classic back-rank weakness. If we could get a queen or rook to e1 it would be checkmate. This gives us the idea – play one of the threatened pieces to the e-file and White will have no time to capture the other piece as doing so will succumb to the checkmate.

So Black can play the flashy 1...Re8, leaving his queen to be taken. This is a perfectly good move. White would deal with the mate threat (perhaps with 2 Be3, blocking the open file), Black would move his queen and the game would go on.

But can Black improve? Yes! **1...Qe6!** This again institutes the mate threat but also sets up another threat, 2...Qxb6. White has no way to both save his knight and prevent the mate. This is a further example of the idea that when you see a good move it is often good to pause and look for a better one.

Exercise 8

This is a tricky one. White has forked the black rook and knight and although Black has various tries to defend the pieces or to instigate counter-threats, only one is successful. Let us look at the various ways to meet this fork:

a) *Move the knight to protect the rook.* Both ways of doing this fail as 1...Ne7? is met by 2 Qxe7 and 1...Ne5? is met by 2 dxe5.

b) *Move the rook to protect the knight.* Black has no method of doing this.

c) *Defend both pieces.* The only way to do this is 1...Qe8. Unfortunately the white queen covers this square and 2 Qxe8+ wins.

d) *Launch a counterattack with the knight.* Unfortunately the knight cannot create any worthwhile threats. 1...Nf4 is a thought as then 2 Qxc6 can be met by 2...Nxe2+. However, White simply takes the knight instead with 2 Qxf4.

e) *Launch a counterattack with the rook.* This looks more promising. Check is the best way to create a threat, but 1...Rc1+ is met by 2 Nxc1. Another try is 1...Rc3, counterattacking against the white knight. Unfortunately White's reply, 2 Qxg6+, is check and Black has no time to capture the white knight.

So, that seems to exhaust all Black's possibilities – must he inevitably lose a piece? When this seems to be the case, you should look for a weakness in the opponent's position which might create a counterchance. Does White have such a weakness here? Yes. His king is on an open file and, as we know, this often creates the chance for a pin. The way for Black to exploit this possibility is with **1...Rc7!**, when **2 Qxg6+** is met by **2...Rg7** and the white queen is pinned against the king.